Easy
Church
Suppers

Hallelujah! Recipes
For One and All

By Barbara C Jones

Easy Church Suppers

1st Printing February 2007

ISBN: 978-1-931294-71-3
Library of Congress Number: 2007921593

Author, Barbara C. Jones
Illustrations by Nancy Bohanan

Edited, Designed and Published in the
United States of America
Manufactured in China

Cookbook Resources, LLC
541 Doubletree Drive
Highland Village, Texas 75077
Toll free 866-229-2665
www.cookbookresources.com

Easy Church Suppers

On the outside we see the churches and the steeples. Then we open the doors and see all the people.

We come to share our common bonds and beliefs that tie us together. It is the "coming together", the sharing of our lives, that makes everyday experiences special and the ordinary times extraordinary.

For church congregations everywhere the church supper is one of the most welcomed and most fun church gatherings on the calendar. It is the "coming together" that everyone enjoys because everyone gets to eat and to visit. How ordinary, but how very extraordinary it is to share our meals with families and friends.

Easy Church Suppers gives you great, easy recipes for every function. Pick-up foods, light suppers for summer evenings, potluck favorites, hearty one-dish meals, dishes to please a crowd and great big homemade cakes, pies and cookies that keep everyone coming back for more and make you a star. And, the best part is you don't have to stay in the kitchen all day to be a star.

These easy recipes use everyday ingredients you probably already have in your pantry. They usually take just a few minutes to put the ingredients together and the cooking is the really easy part. **And after you make them and bake them, it's easy to take them.**

Enjoy your church suppers with these quick-and-easy, delicious recipes for every gathering. And enjoy the "coming together" and the sharing that makes church suppers not ordinary, but extraordinary.

Editor's Choice Recipes

Contents

Summer Suppers

Perfect punches, casual pick-up foods, exotic sandwiches, hearty salads and scrumptious desserts that call for "seconds".

Beverages 8

Appetizers 11

Sandwiches 13

Salads 16

Desserts.. 37

Make, Bake and Take

Delicious and "fancy" main dishes, favorite vegetable dishes, pleasing and practical breads, tasty pasta and splendid cakes and pies.

Chicken... 46

Beef.. 84

Pork 98

Seafood 113

Breads 115

Vegetables 125

Side Dishes.. 147

Cakes... 162

Pies.. 165

Contents

4-Ingredient Fast Fixes
76 fast, easy 4-ingredient dishes to get you to the church on time! ... Favorites for last-minute and hurry-up covered dishes.

Main Dishes 172

Vegetables, Sides and Breads 190

Salads 202

Desserts 208

Crowd Pleasers
Fabulous recipes for groups of 20... Easy on planners and cooks – Expecting 40? Make 2... 60? Make 3...It's that easy!

Vegetables and Side Dishes.................... 212

Chicken... 221

Beef... 227

Pork 230

Seafood 234

Desserts.. 236

Index... 243

Cookbooks Published............................... 254

Order Form 255

Summer Suppers

Perfect punches, casual pick-up foods, exotic sandwiches, hearty salads and scrumptious desserts that call for "seconds".

Beverages 8

Appetizers 11

Sandwiches 13

Salads 16

Desserts 37

Green Party Punch

This punch is good for St. Patrick's Day or any day.

1 (3 ounce) package lime gelatin
1 (6 ounce) can frozen limeade, thawed
1 (6 ounce) can frozen lemonade, thawed
1 quart orange juice
1 quart pineapple juice
1 tablespoon almond extract
2 - 3 drops green food coloring
1 liter ginger ale, chilled

- Dissolve lime gelatin and 1 cup boiling water and stir well.
- In 1-gallon bottle, combine dissolved gelatin, limeade, lemonade, orange juice, pineapple juice, almond extract and food coloring and chill.
- When ready to serve, add ginger ale. Serves 32.

Very Special Coffee Punch

This will be a hit! It is great!

1 (2 ounce) jar instant coffee
2¼ cups sugar
2 quarts half-and-half cream
1 quart ginger ale
1 pint whipping cream, whipped
½ gallon French vanilla ice cream

- Dissolve instant coffee in 2 quarts hot water and cool.
- Add sugar and cream, mix well and chill.
- When ready to serve, pour coffee-sugar mixture in punch bowl, add chilled ginger ale, whipped cream and ice cream. Let some chunks of ice cream remain. Serves 60 (4 ounce).

A heart at piece gives root to the body, but envy rots the bones. Proverbs 14:30

Holiday Party Punch

The almond extract really gives this punch a special taste!

3 cups sugar
1 (6 ounce) package lemon gelatin
1 (3 ounce) can frozen orange juice concentrate, thawed
⅓ cup lemon juice
1 (46 ounce) can pineapple juice
3 tablespoons almond extract
2 quarts ginger ale, chilled

- Combine sugar and 1-quart water. Heat until sugar dissolves.
- Add gelatin and stir until it dissolves. Add fruit juices, 1½ quarts water and almond extract and chill.
- When ready to serve, place in punch bowl and add chilled ginger ale. Serves 50.

 # Reception Punch

4 cups sugar
5 ripe bananas, mashed
Juice of 2 lemons
1 (46 ounce) can pineapple juice
1 (6 ounce) can frozen orange juice concentrate, thawed
2 quarts ginger ale

- Boil sugar and 6 cups water for 3 minutes and cool.
- Blend bananas with lemon juice and add pineapple and orange juice. Combine all ingredients except ginger ale. Freeze in large container.
- To serve, thaw 1½ hours, then add ginger ale. Punch will be slushy. Serves 40.

Let no debt remain outstanding. Romans 13:8

Ruby Holiday Punch

The cranapple juice in this punch really makes it a "holiday" special!

2 (6 ounce) cans frozen orange juice concentrate, thawed
2 (46 ounce) cans red Hawaiian punch
1 (46 ounce) can pineapple juice
1 (48 ounce) bottle cranapple juice
2 liters ginger ale, chilled

- In 2-gallon bottles, combine orange juice, 4 cups water, Hawaiian punch, pineapple juice and cranapple juice and stir well.
- Chill and place in punch bowl.
- Just before serving, add ginger ale. Makes 2 gallons.

Sparkling Cranberry Punch

Red food coloring (optional)
2 quarts cranberry juice cocktail
1 (6 ounce) can frozen lemonade, thawed
1 quart ginger ale, chilled

- Pour water in ice mold for ice ring and add a little red food coloring for a brighter look.
- Mix cranberry juice and lemonade in pitcher. Chill until ready to serve.
- When ready to serve, pour cranberry mixture into punch bowl, add ginger ale and stir well.
- Add decorative ice mold to punch bowl. Yields 24 cups.

Let us learn together what is good. Job 34:4

Cheesy Vegetable Squares

1 (8 ounce) package refrigerated crescent rolls
1 (8 ounce) package cream cheese, softened
½ cup mayonnaise
1 (1.4 ounce) packet ranch salad dressing mix
1 cup prepared broccoli slaw
1½ cups shredded cheddar cheese

- Preheat oven to 350°.

- Press crescent roll dough into 9 x 13-inch baking dish and press perforations to seal. Bake for 12 minutes or until dough is golden brown; cool.

- With mixer, beat cream cheese, mayonnaise and ranch dressing mix; spread over crust. Sprinkle with broccoli slaw and top with cheese; gently press into cream cheese mixture. Cover and chill at least 3 hours. Cut into squares to serve. Serves 6.

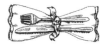

Ask, and it shall be given to you; seek, and ye shall find: knock, and it shall be open unto you. Matthew 7:7

Orange-Glazed Chicken Wings

3 pounds chicken wings
1¼ cups soy sauce
1¼ cups orange juice
1 cup packed brown sugar
1 teaspoon minced garlic

- Dry wings with paper towels. In large sealable bag, combine soy sauce, orange juice, brown sugar and garlic. Place wings in bag and seal. Refrigerate overnight.

- Preheat oven to 325°. Drain wings and discard marinade.

- Place wings in sprayed, foil-lined 10 x 15-inch baking pan.

- Bake for 45 minutes, or until wings are light brown and glazed. Turn once while baking. Serves 8 to 10.

Chili-Honey Wings

1½ cups flour
18 - 20 wing drummettes and wing portions
¼ cup (½ stick) butter
¾ cup honey
⅔ cup chili sauce

- Preheat oven to 325°.

- Combine flour and a little salt in shallow bowl and dredge each wing portion in flour. Melt butter in large skillet and brown 5 to 6 wings at one time on medium-high heat . When brown, place in sprayed 9 x 13-inch baking pan.

- In small bowl, combine honey and chili sauce and mix well. Spoon honey mixture over each wing. Cover and bake for 45 minutes. Serves 6 to 10.

Cheesy Black Olive Sandwiches

2 (8 ounce) packages cream cheese, softened
¼ cup mayonnaise
1 (4 ounce) can chopped black olives
¾ cup finely chopped pecans
Pumpernickel rye or party rye bread

- With mixer, beat cream cheese and mayonnaise until creamy. Stir in chopped olives and pecans. (If mixture seems too stiff to spread, add 1 tablespoon mayonnaise.)
- Spread mixture on slices of pumpernickel rye bread or on 3-inch squares of party rye bread. If pumpernickel is used, slice sandwiches into 3 finger strips. Serves 8 to 12.

Guacamole-Ham Wrap

¾ cup prepared guacamole
4 (8 inch) spinach tortillas
¾ cup salsa
½ (8 ounce) package shredded 4-cheese blend
¾ pound deli ham, cut in thin strips
Shredded lettuce

- Spread guacamole over half of each tortilla and layer salsa, cheese, ham strips and lettuce to within 2 inches of edges. Roll tightly. Refrigerate. Serves 4.

Let your gentleness be evident to all … Do not be anxious about anything.
Philippians 4:5, 6

Chicken-Bacon Sandwiches

1 (12 ounce) can chicken breast, drained
⅓ cup mayonnaise
1 tablespoon dijon-style mustard
1 celery rib, finely chopped
3 tablespoons finely diced green onions
¼ cup cooked, crumbled bacon
Shredded lettuce

- In medium bowl, combine chicken chunks, mayonnaise, mustard, celery, green onions, bacon and a little salt and pepper.
- Spread chicken mixture on whole wheat or white bread (crust removed) and top with shredded lettuce. Place second slice of bread on top and cut to make 4 little "bites". Serves 4 to 8.

Party Sandwich Strips

1 (4 ounce) package pre-cooked crumbled bacon
½ cup ripe olives, chopped
½ cup chopped pecans
1¼ cups mayonnaise

- In bowl, combine bacon, olives, pecans, mayonnaise and a little salt and pepper. Spread mixture on thin slices of white bread and cut sandwiches into three strips. Serves 8 to 12.

TIP: These ingredients can be spread on croissants and baked for 5 minutes at 350°.

Finally, all of you, live in harmony with one another, be sympathetic, love as brothers, be compassionate and humble. First Peter 3:8

Turkey On A Muffin

4 slices Swiss cheese
2 English muffins, split, toasted
½ pound thinly sliced deli turkey
1 (15 ounce) can asparagus spears, well drained
1 (1 ounce) packet hollandaise sauce mix
Butter

- Place cheese slice on each muffin half and top with turkey slices. Cut asparagus spears to fit muffin halves and top each sandwich with 3 or 4 asparagus spears. (Use remaining asparagus for another use.)
- Prepare hollandaise sauce according to package directions and pour generous amount over each open-face sandwich. Serve immediately. Serves 4.

Turkey-Cranberry Croissants

1 (8 ounce) package cream cheese, softened
½ cup orange marmalade
6 large croissants, split
Shredded lettuce
1 pound thinly sliced deli turkey
1 cup whole berry cranberry sauce

- With mixer, beat cream cheese, orange marmalade and 1 tablespoon water. Spread small amount evenly on cut sides of croissants.
- Top with lettuce and slices of turkey. Place cranberry sauce in bowl and stir for easy spreading. Spread 2 or 3 tablespoons cranberries over turkey and place top of croissant over cranberry sauce. Serves 6.

Love is patient, love is kind. First Corinthians 13:4

Colorful English Pea Salad

2 (16 ounce) packages frozen green peas, thawed, drained
1 (8 ounce) package cubed mozzarella cheese
1 red and 1 orange bell pepper, seeded, chopped
1 small red onion, cut in rings
2 eggs, hard-boiled, chopped
1¼ cups mayonnaise
1 teaspoon seasoned salt
1 teaspoon seasoned pepper
⅓ cup cooked, crumbled bacon

- In large salad bowl, combine uncooked peas, cheese, bell peppers, onion rings and chopped eggs. Stir in mayonnaise, salt and pepper.
- Refrigerate and when ready to serve, garnish with crumbled bacon. Serves 8 to 10.

Black Bean & Mandarin Salad

1 (15 ounce) can beans, rinsed, drained
1 (11 ounce) can mandarin oranges, well drained
1 cup finely diced jicama
¼ cup finely diced red onion
¼ cup finely diced jalapeno
½ (8 ounce) bottle zesty Italian dressing

- In large bowl, combine all ingredients, refrigerate until ready to serve and toss occasionally. Serves 6 to 8.

Whoever does not love does not know God, because God is love.
First John 4:8

Cauliflower-Bacon Salad

1 large head cauliflower, cut into florets
1 red and 1 green bell pepper, seeded, chopped
1½ cups cubed mozzarella cheese
1 (6 ounce) package cooked, crumbled bacon
1 bunch fresh green onions, sliced

- In plastic bowl with lid, combine cauliflower, bell peppers, cheese, crumbled bacon and green onions.

Dressing:
1 cup mayonnaise
1 tablespoon sugar
1 tablespoon lemon juice

- In small bowl, combine mayonnaise, sugar, lemon juice and 1 teaspoon seasoned salt and a little black pepper; mix well. Spoon dressing over salad and toss to coat. Cover and refrigerate several hours before serving. Serves 6 to 8.

Choice Broccoli-Swiss Salad

2 large bunches fresh broccoli, washed, drained
1 (8 ounce) carton fresh mushrooms, sliced
1 (8 ounce) block Swiss cheese, diced
1 (3 ounce) package sliced pepperoni, chopped
1 (8 ounce) carton cherry tomatoes, halved, drained
1 (8 ounce) bottle zesty Italian salad dressing

- Cut broccoli into florets, discard stems and place in plastic bowl with lid. Add mushrooms, diced cheese, pepperoni and tomatoes. Toss with Italian salad dressing and refrigerate. Serves 8.

And God shall wipe away every tear from their eyes. Revelation 7:17

Macaroni-Vegetable Salad

1 (16 ounce) package tri-colored macaroni
1 sweet red bell pepper, seeded, julienned
1 small zucchini, sliced
2 cups small broccoli floret
1 cup refrigerated Caesar salad dressing

- Cook macaroni according to package directions and drain.
  Place in container with lid and add bell pepper, zucchini,
  broccoli and a little salt and pepper.

- Toss with salad dressing. Use more if needed to coat salad
  well. Cover and refrigerate several hours before serving.
  Serves 6 to 8.

Great Carrot Salad

1 (16 ounce) package shredded carrots
1 (8 ounce) package crushed pineapple, drained
⅓ cup chopped pecans
3 tablespoons flaked coconut
½ cup mayonnaise

- Combine carrots, pineapple, pecans, coconut and mayonnaise. Mix well and refrigerate. Serves 6 to 8.

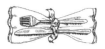

Honor the Lord with your wealth, with the first fruits of all your crops.
Proverbs 3:9

Classic Apple-Cranberry Salad

Dressing:
½ cup mayonnaise
2 tablespoons peanut butter
1 teaspoon lemon juice
½ teaspoon sugar

- In salad bowl, whisk together mayonnaise, peanut butter, lemon juice and sugar.

Salad:
2 gala apples with peel, chopped
2 celery ribs, chopped
⅓ cup cherry-flavored Craisins®
1 cup shredded lettuce
¼ cup chopped pecans

- Add apples, celery and Craisins® and toss to coat well. Cover and refrigerate about 1 hour.
- Arrange lettuce on serving platter, top with chilled apple mixture and sprinkle evenly with pecans. Serves 4 to 6.

Best when you pray, go into your room, close the door and pray to your Father who is unseen.   Matthew 6:6

Couscous Salad

1 (5.6 ounce) box parmesan couscous
¾ cup chopped fresh mushrooms
1 (4 ounce) can sliced ripe olives, drained
½ cup green bell pepper
½ cup red bell pepper
½ cup Italian salad dressing

- Cook couscous according to package directions. Cover and let stand 5 minutes, then fluff with fork.
- In salad bowl, combine couscous, mushrooms, olives and bell peppers.
- Stir in salad dressing, cover and refrigerate 30 minutes before serving. Serves 6.

Orange-Cranberry Salad

1 (10 ounce) package red-tipped lettuce, rinsed
1 seedless cucumber, halved lengthwise, sliced
1 (11 ounce) can mandarin oranges, drained
½ cup Craisins®
⅓ cup toasted slivered almonds, toasted
1 (12 ounce) bottle raspberry-vinaigrette dressing

- In salad bowl, combine lettuce, cucumber, oranges, Craisins® and almonds. Toss with about one-third of dressing; use more as needed. Serves 6 to 8.

Rejoice in the Lord always. Philippians 4:4

Green Salad with Candied Pecans

Candied pecans:
1⅓ cups pecan halves
¼ cup honey
3 tablespoon light corn syrup

- Preheat oven to 325°.
- Combine pecans, honey and corn syrup in bowl and stir until pecans are well coated.
- Spread out on rimmed baking sheet and bake for 12 minutes or until pecans toast. Remove to piece of foil, separate clumps with fork and cool.

Salad:
1 (10 ounce) package baby spinach
4 cups young salad greens
1 tart apple, seeded, thinly sliced
1 cup crumbled blue cheese
1 (8 ounce) bottle zesty Italian salad dressing

- In salad bowl, combine spinach, greens, apple slices and blue cheese; toss with about half bottle of salad dressing. Add more if needed.
- Sprinkle candied pecans over top of salad when ready to serve. Serves 8 to 10.

Jesus wept. John 11:35

Great Chicken 'N Greens Salad

2 cups skinned, diced rotisserie chicken
1 (10 ounce) package mixed greens
½ cup chopped sun-dried tomatoes
1 red bell pepper, seeded, chopped
3 tablespoons sunflower seeds

- In salad bowl, combine chicken, greens, tomatoes and bell pepper and toss.

Dressing:
½ (8 ounce) bottle vinaigrette salad dressing
2 tablespoons refrigerated honey-mustard salad dressing

- Combine vinaigrette dressing and honey-mustard dressing, pour over salad and toss. (Use more dressing if needed.) Sprinkle sunflower seeds over salad and serve. Serves 6 to 8.

Spinach-Strawberry Salad

1 (10 ounce) package fresh spinach, stems removed
½ small jicama, peeled, cut into very slender strips
½ yellow bell pepper, seeded, chopped
2 cups fresh bean sprouts
1 pint fresh strawberries, stemmed, halved
1 (8 ounce) bottle poppy seed dressing

- Combine spinach, jicama, bell pepper and bean sprouts in salad bowl.
- When ready to serve, add strawberries and about half poppy seed dressing. Use more if needed and toss. Serves 8.

…let every man be swift to hear, slow to speak, slow to wrath. James 1:19

Nutty Rice Salad

1 (6 ounce) package long-grain and wild rice mix
1 (6 ounce) jar marinated artichoke hearts, drained, chopped
1 cup golden raisins
4 fresh green onions with tops, chopped
¾ cup pecan halves, toasted

- Prepare rice mix according to package directions, drain and cool. Place in salad bowl and add artichoke hearts, raisins and green onions.

Dressing:
⅓ cup orange juice
¼ cup olive oil
1 tablespoon lemon juice
1 tablespoon sugar

- For dressing, combine orange juice, oil, lemon juice and sugar. Stir dressing until they blend well, spoon over salad and toss.
- Cover and refrigerate at least 2 hours; top with pecans before serving. Serves 6 to 8.

TIP: Pecans can be toasted at 300° for 10 minutes. You don't have to toast pecans, but it sure brings out the flavor.

Thy word is a lamp to my feet and a light for my path. Psalm 119:105

Pasta Plus Salad

1 (16 ounce) package bow-tie pasta
1 (10 ounce) package frozen green peas, thawed
1 red bell pepper, seeded, cut in strips
1 (8 ounce) package cubed Swiss cheese
1 small yellow summer squash, sliced

- Cook pasta according to package directions and add peas last 2 minutes of cooking time. Drain pasta and peas, rinse in cold water and drain again. Transfer to large salad bowl.

Dressing:

¾ cup mayonnaise
2 tablespoons lemon juice
1 tablespoon sugar
½ cup whipping cream

- Combine dressing ingredients and mix well. Spoon over salad with a little salt and pepper. Toss salad and refrigerate several hours before serving. Serves 8.

Pasta-Veggie Salad

1 (16 ounce) package corkscrew pasta
1 (16 ounce) package frozen broccoli-cauliflower, thawed
1 (8 ounce) block mozzarella cheese, cubed
1 (8 ounce) bottle Catalina salad dressing

- Cook pasta according to package directions, drain and cool. Cook vegetables in microwave according to package directions, drain and cool.
- In large bowl, combine pasta, vegetables and cheese and toss with salad dressing. Chill before serving. Serves 10.

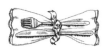

Tri-color Pasta Salad

3 cups tri-color spiral pasta
1 tablespoon olive oil
1 large bunch broccoli, cut into small florets
1 cup chopped celery
1 cup peeled, thinly sliced cucumber
1 (1 pound) block Swiss cheese, cubed
1 (8 ounce) bottle ranch dressing

- Cook pasta according to package directions and drain. Stir in olive oil and transfer to large salad bowl. Add broccoli florets, celery, cucumber, cheese and a little salt and pepper.
- Pour dressing over salad and toss. Chill several hours for flavors to blend. Serves 10.

Deviled Eggs

8 - 10 eggs, hard-boiled
¼ cup sweet pickle relish
1 (4 ounce) can chopped pimento, drained
½ cup chopped pecans
⅓ cup mayonnaise
Paprika

- Peel eggs and cut in half lengthwise. Remove yolks and mash with fork. Add relish, pimento, pecans, mayonnaise and a little salt and pepper. Add more mayonnaise if needed.
- Place yolk mixture back into egg white halves. Sprinkle with paprika and refrigerate. Serves 6 to 10.

A friend loveth at all times. Proverbs 17:17

Zesty Bean Salad

1 (15 ounce) can kidney beans, rinsed, drained
1 (15 ounce) can pinto beans, rinsed, drained
1 (15 ounce) can whole kernel corn, drained
1 red bell pepper, seeded, chopped
1 red onion, chopped
1 (7 ounce) can chopped green chilies
1 (12 ounce) package cubed Mexican 4-cheese blend

- In large bowl, combine both beans, corn, bell pepper, onion, green chilies and cheese; mix well.

Dressing:
1 (8 ounce) bottle cheddar-parmesan ranch dressing
2 tablespoons lemon juice
1 teaspoon Creole seasoning

- Pour ranch dressing into bowl and stir in lemon juice and seasoning. Pour over salad and toss. Refrigerate several hours before serving for flavors to blend. Serves 10 to 12.

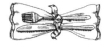

But those who hope in the Lord will renew their strength. They will soar on wings like eagles, they will run and not grow weary, they will walk and not be faint. Isaiah 40:31

Oriental Spinach Salad

1 (10 ounce) package fresh spinach, stems removed
2 eggs, hard-boiled, sliced
1 cup fresh bean sprouts
1 (8 ounce) can sliced water chestnuts
1 red bell pepper, seeded, chopped

- In salad bowl, combine spinach, eggs, bean sprouts, water chestnuts and bell pepper.

Oriental Dressing:
¾ cup olive oil
¼ cup sugar
¼ cup ketchup
3 tablespoons red wine vinegar

- Place all dressing ingredients in jar with lid and shake well to blend.
- When ready to serve, pour about half dressing over salad (use more if needed) and toss. Serves 6.

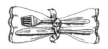

A man of many companions may come to ruin, but there is a friend who sticks closer than a brother. Proverbs 18:24

Spinach Salad with Warm Bacon Dressing

1 (10 ounce) package fresh spinach, stems removed
3 eggs, hard-boiled, chopped
1 (8 ounce) carton fresh mushrooms, sliced
3 fresh green onions, sliced

- Combine spinach, eggs, mushrooms and onions in salad bowl.

Hot Bacon Dressing:

6 slices bacon
½ cup sugar
½ cup apple cider vinegar
2 tablespoons cornstarch

- Fry bacon in skillet until crisp and drain on paper towel. Leave bacon drippings in skillet. Crumble bacon and set aside.
- In saucepan with bacon drippings, combine sugar, vinegar, ¼ cup water and cornstarch in saucepan. Bring mixture to a boil, stirring constantly until mixture is thick.
- Add crumbled bacon to salad and toss with about three-fourths of hot bacon dressing. Add more if needed. Serve immediately. Serves 8.

To everything there is a season, and a time to every purpose.
Ecclesiastes 3:1

Swiss Romaine

1 large head romaine lettuce, torn into bite-size pieces
1 bunch fresh green onions with tops, sliced
1 sweet red bell pepper, seeded, julienned
1 (8 ounce) package shredded Swiss cheese
⅓ cup sunflower seeds
Seasoned croutons

- Combine romaine, green onions, bell pepper and shredded cheese in salad bowl.

Vinaigrette Dressing:
⅔ cup olive oil
⅓ cup red wine vinegar
2 teaspoons sugar

- In jar with lid, combine oil, vinegar and sugar and shake well. Add sunflower seeds to salad and toss with vinaigrette dressing. Sprinkle croutons over top of salad. Serves 8.

Special Cauliflower Salad

1 head cauliflower, cut into bite-size pieces
1 (10 ounce) package frozen green peas, thawed
1 sweet red bell pepper, seeded, chopped
1 small purple onion, chopped
1 (8 ounce) carton sour cream
1 (1 ounce) packet dry ranch-style salad dressing

- In large salad bowl, combine cauliflower, peas, bell pepper and chopped onion. Combine sour cream and ranch dressing and toss with vegetables. Refrigerate. Serves 8.

Therefore, as we have opportunity, let us do good to all people. Galatians 6:10

Ranch Potato Salad

2 pounds red (new) potatoes
1 (8 ounce) block mozzarella cheese, cubed
2 ribs celery, sliced
1 red bell pepper, seeded, chopped
1 (2.8 ounce) package bacon bits
1 (8 ounce) bottle ranch salad dressing

- Place potatoes in large saucepan with water to cover and bring to a boil. Reduce heat and simmer about 20 minutes or until potatoes are tender. Drain and allow to cool just enough to be able to cube.

- Place potatoes in large salad bowl and add cheese, celery, bell pepper, bacon bits and a little salt and pepper. Pour salad dressing over salad and toss. Refrigerate at least 2 hours before serving. Serves 10 to 12.

Brown Rice Chicken Salad

1 (8.8 ounce) package whole-grain brown rice
1 (12 ounce) can premium chunk chicken breasts, drained
⅔ cup chopped sun-dried tomatoes
2 ripe avocados, peeled, diced
¾ cup dijon-style mustard vinaigrette dressing

- Prepare rice according to package directions. (Microwave in package.) Combine rice, chicken, tomatoes, avocados and a little salt and pepper.

- Spoon dressing over salad and gently toss to mix well. Refrigerate at least 2 hours before serving. Serves 8.

From birth I have relied on you. Psalm 71:6

Chicken-Waldorf Salad

1 pound boneless, skinless chicken breast, halves
1 red and 1 green apple with peel, sliced
1 cup sliced celery
¾ cup chopped walnuts
2 (6 ounce) cartons orange yogurt
½ cup mayonnaise
1 teaspoon seasoned salt
Shredded lettuce

- Place chicken in large saucepan and cover with water. On high heat, cook about 15 minutes, drain and cool. Cut into 1-inch chunks and season with salt and pepper. Place in large salad bowl.

- Add sliced apples, celery and walnuts. Mix yogurt, mayonnaise and seasoned salt well. Toss with chicken-apple mixture. This salad may be served at room temperature or chilled several hours. Serve over shredded lettuce. Serves 8.

Special Romaine Salad

1 large head romaine lettuce
1 sweet red bell pepper, seeded, julienned
1 seedless cucumber, peeled, sliced
1 (3 ounce) package bacon bits
¾ cup shredded Swiss cheese
1 (8 ounce) bottle creamy Italian dressing
2 tablespoons sesame seeds

- Tear lettuce into bite-size pieces and place in salad bowl. Add bell pepper, cucumber, bacon and Swiss cheese and toss.

- When ready to serve, use a little more than half the dressing, or more if needed and toss. Sprinkle with sesame seeds. Serves 8 to 10.

Turkey-Apple Salad

1 pound deli turkey, coarsely shredded
2 tart green apples, peeled, chopped
½ cup chopped pitted dates
3 ribs celery, sliced

- Combine all ingredients in large salad bowl.

Dressing:
⅔ cup walnut halves, toasted
⅓ cup sour cream
½ cup mayonnaise
1 tablespoon lemon juice

- In bowl, combine sour cream, mayonnaise, lemon juice and a little salt and pepper and mix well. Stir in walnuts.
- Combine all salad ingredients and toss with dressing. Serves 8.

Chilled Cinnamon Salad

1 cup cinnamon red hot candies
1 (6 ounce) package cherry gelatin
1 (24 ounce) jar applesauce
1 cup chopped pecans
Shredded lettuce

- Heat cinnamon red hots in 1 cup boiling water until candy melts. While mixture is still hot, pour over gelatin and mix well. Add applesauce and chopped pecans, mix well.
- Pour into 7 x 11-inch glass dish and refrigerate several hours or until firm. Cut into squares and serve each square over shredded lettuce. Serves 8.

Turkey-Black Bean Salad

1 pound deli turkey, coarsely chopped
2 (15 ounce) cans black beans, rinsed, drained
1 bunch fresh green onions, sliced
1 sweet bell pepper, seeded, chopped

- In bowl, combine chopped turkey, beans, green onions and bell pepper.

Cumin Vinaigrette:
¾ cup virgin olive oil
¼ cup lemon juice
2 teaspoons ground cumin
2 teaspoons sugar

- In small jar with lid, combine all vinaigrette ingredients, plus a little salt and pepper. Shake well to blend ingredients. Spoon over salad and toss. Refrigerate several hours. Serves 8.

No-Trouble Fruit Salad

2 (20 ounce) cans peach pie filling
1 (16 ounce) carton fresh strawberries, halved
3 bananas, sliced
1 (20 ounce) can pineapple tidbits, drained

- Place pie filling in container with lid; add strawberries, bananas and pineapple and gently mix. Cover and refrigerate.
- Place in crystal bowl to serve. Serves 10.

Tip: Substitute apricot pie filling for the peach pie filling if you prefer apricots.

He has sent me to bind up the brokenhearted. Isaiah 61:1

Mango Salad Supreme

1 (6 ounce) package orange gelatin
1 (8 ounce) package cream cheese, softened
2 (15 ounce) cans mangoes with juice
2 (11 ounce) cans mandarin oranges, drained
1 (8 ounce) carton whipped topping

- Place gelatin in mixing bowl, pour 1 cup boiling water over gelatin and mix well. Cool about 30 minutes. Cut cream cheese into chunks and add to mixing bowl with gelatin. With mixer at a very slow speed at first, beat in cream cheese.

- Fold in mangoes and oranges and chill until just partially congealed. Fold in whipped topping, spoon into 9 x 13-inch glass dish and refrigerate several hours. Serves 8.

Cranberry-Cherry Salad

1 (6 ounce) package cherry gelatin
1 (20 ounce) can cherry pie filling
1 (16 ounce) can whole cranberry sauce
¾ cup chopped pecans

- Combine cherry gelatin with 1 cup boiling water and mix until gelatin dissolves. Stir in pie filling, cranberry sauce and pecans and mix until they blend well.

- Pour into 7 x 11-inch glass dish and refrigerate several hours until it congeals Serves 8.

Do not judge, or you too will be judged. Matthew 7:1

Broccoli Slaw

1 (16 ounce) package broccoli slaw
1 cup small fresh broccoli florets
¾ cup Craisins®
1 Granny Smith apple with peel, diced
1 (11 ounce) can mandarin oranges, well drained
1 (8 ounce) bottle poppy seed dressing
½ cup slivered almonds, toasted

- In salad bowl, combine broccoli slaw, broccoli florets, Craisins®, apple and oranges. Toss with poppy seed dressing.
- Sprinkle almonds on top of salad. Refrigerate at least 2 hours before serving. Serves 8.

Cabbage-Carrot Slaw

1 (16 ounce) package shredded carrots
3 cups shredded cabbage
2 red delicious apples with peel, diced
¾ cup raisins
¾ cup chopped walnuts
1 (8 ounce) bottle cold slaw dressing

- In plastic bowl with lid, combine shredded carrots, shredded cabbage, apples, raisins and walnuts.
- Add about three-fourths bottle of slaw dressing and increase dressing if needed. Cover and refrigerate several hours before serving. Serves 8.

God is light; in him there is no darkness at all. First John 1:5

Citrus-Broccoli Slaw

1 (16 ounce) package broccoli slaw
1 small jicama, peeled, julienned
2 (11 ounce) cans mandarin oranges, drained
1 small red onion, halved, thinly sliced
⅔ cup fresh chopped cilantro

- In bowl, combine broccoli slaw, jicama, oranges, onion and cilantro and mix well.

Dressing:
3 tablespoons olive oil
3 tablespoons lemon juice
1½ tablespoons sugar
1½ teaspoons grated orange peel

- Combine all dressing ingredients in container with lid. Shake well, pour over salad and toss. Serves 6 to 8.

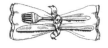

And God is able to make all grace abound to you, so that in all things at all times, having all that you need, you will abound in every good work. Second Corinthians 9:8

Chocolate-Fudge Brownies

4 (1 ounce) unsweetened chocolate baking squares
1 cup (2 sticks) butter, softened
2 cups sugar
4 large eggs, slightly beaten
1 cup flour
1 teaspoon vanilla
1 cup semi-sweet chocolate chips
⅔ cup chopped pecans

- Preheat oven to 350°.

- Microwave chocolate squares in microwave-safe bowl on MEDIUM power for 90 seconds. Stir at 30-second intervals until chocolate melts and is smooth.

- In mixing bowl, beat butter and sugar at medium speed until light and fluffy. Add eggs, 1 at a time, and beat after each addition. Add melted chocolate and beat well. Add flour and beat on low speed. Stir in vanilla, chocolate chips and pecans.

- Spread batter into sprayed, floured 9 x 13-inch baking pan. Bake for 35 to 40 minutes or until center is set. Cool completely on wire rack and cut into squares. Serves 10 to 14.

TIP: To easily remove and cut brownies, line pan with sprayed, floured heavy-duty foil and allow several inches to extend over sides. After baking and cooling, lift block of brownies from the pan using foil. Press foil sides down and cut into squares.

In everything set them an example by doing what is good. Titus 2:7

Cheesecake Squares

1 (8 ounce) carton sour cream
1 (8 ounce) package cream cheese, softened
1 (3.4 ounce) package instant French vanilla pudding
⅓ cup milk
1 (8 ounce) carton whipped topping
1 (20 ounce) can pineapple pie filling

- With mixer, beat sour cream and cream cheese until creamy. Stir in pudding and milk and mix well. Fold in whipped topping and spoon into 9 x 13-inch dish. Chill about 15 minutes.

- Spoon pineapple pie filling over top using back of large spoon to spread filling evenly. Refrigerate at least 3 hours before cutting into squares to serve. Serves 8 to 10.

Apple Crescents

1 (8 ounce) can refrigerated crescent rolls
2 Granny Smith apples, peeled, quartered
1 cup orange juice
1¼ cups sugar
½ cup (1 stick) butter
1 teaspoon cinnamon

- Preheat oven to 350°.
- Unroll crescent rolls and separate. Wrap each apple quarter with crescent roll. Place each apple crescent in sprayed 9 x 13-inch baking dish.
- In saucepan, combine orange juice, sugar, butter and cinnamon and bring to a boil. Pour over crescents and bake for 30 minutes or until golden and bubbly. Serves 8.

Peanut Butter-Toffee Bars

1 (18 ounce) box yellow cake mix
1 cup crunchy peanut butter
2 eggs
1 (8 ounce) package milk chocolate-toffee bits
½ cup chopped peanuts
1 (12 ounce) package milk chocolate chips

- Preheat oven to 350°.

- Spray, flour bottom and sides of 10 x 15-inch baking pan.

- In large bowl, combine cake mix, peanut butter, ½ cup water and eggs with spoon. Stir in toffee bits and peanuts and spread evenly in pan.

- Bake for 25 minutes then immediately sprinkle chocolate chips over hot bars. Let stand about 5 minutes or until chips melt. With back of spoon spread chocolate evenly. Cool completely before cutting into bars. Serves 6 to 10.

A cheerful heart is good medicine, but a crushed spirit dries up the bones.
Proverbs 17:22

Peanut Brittle Bars

2¼ cups flour
⅔ cup packed brown sugar
¾ cup (1½ sticks) butter, softened
1 (16 ounce) jar cocktail peanuts
1 (6 ounce) package milk chocolate pieces
1 (12 ounce) jar caramel ice cream topping
3 tablespoons flour

- Preheat oven to 350°. Line 10 x 15-inch baking pan with foil. Spray foil and set aside.

- In bowl, combine flour and brown sugar. Use pastry blender to cut in butter until mixture is crumbly. Press mixture onto bottom of pan and bake for 12 minutes.

- Sprinkle peanuts and milk chocolate pieces over warm crust. In small bowl, stir caramel topping and 3 tablespoons flour and drizzle over top.

- Return to oven for 13 to 15 minutes more or until caramel bubbles. Cool. Carefully lift foil and gently peel foil away from edges. Cut into bars. Serves 8 to 14.

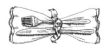

The Lord will fight for you; you need only be still. Exodus 14:14

Pecan Squares

2 cups flour
¾ cup powdered sugar
1¼ cups (2½ sticks), divided plus 2 tablespoons butter, softened
½ cup packed brown sugar
½ cup corn syrup
3 tablespoons whipping cream
3 cups coarsely chopped pecans

- Preheat oven to 350°.

- Sift flour and powdered sugar. Cut in ¾ cup (1½ sticks) butter with pastry blender until mixture resembles coarse meal.

- Pat mixture on bottom and 1½ inches up sides of sprayed 9 x 13-inch baking pan. Bake for 20 minutes or until edges are light brown. Cool.

- In saucepan, bring brown sugar, corn syrup, ½ cup (1 stick) plus 2 tablespoons butter and whipping cream to a rolling boil over medium-high heat. Stir in pecans and pour into baked crust.

- Bake for 25 to 30 minutes or until golden. Cool completely before slicing into squares. Serves 10 to 16.

For there is a proper time and procedure for every matter.
Ecclesiastes 8:6

Decadent Oatmeal Cookies

1 cup (2 sticks) butter, softened
1 cup packed brown sugar
⅔ cup sugar
1½ teaspoons baking soda
2 eggs
1 teaspoon vanilla
2¼ cups flour
2 cups rolled oats
1 cup coarsely chopped cashews
1 cup white chocolate chips
⅔ cup butterscotch chips

- Preheat oven to 375°.

- In mixing bowl, combine and beat butter, brown sugar, sugar, baking soda and ½ teaspoon salt. Beat in eggs and vanilla until they blend well.

- Beat in as much flour as possible with mixer and stir by hand any remaining flour, oats, cashews, white chocolate and butterscotch chips.

- Drop rounded teaspoons of dough 2 inches apart onto unsprayed baking sheet. Bake for 8 to 10 minutes or until edges are golden. Cool on wire rack. Serves 12 to 16.

This is love for God: to obey His commandments. First John 5:3

Pecan Tassies

Crust:
½ cup (1 stick) butter, softened
2 (3 ounce) packages cream cheese, softened
2 cups flour

- Preheat oven to 375°.
- Beat together butter and cream cheese until smooth. Stir in flour until they blend well. Refrigerate at least 30 to 45 minutes.
- Divide dough into 24 equal pieces, flatten each into 3-inch round and fit into 24 mini muffin cups. Let dough extend slightly above each cup.

Filling:
3 eggs, slightly beaten
¼ cup (½ stick) butter, melted
2 cups packed brown sugar
1 cup chopped pecans

- Combine all filling ingredients and spoon about 1 table-spoon into each cup. Bake for 20 minutes or until pastry is light brown and filling is set. Serves 6 to 8.

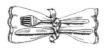

Blessed is the man who perseveres under trial ... he will receive a crown of life.
James 1:12

Chocolate Bread Pudding

1 (3 ounce) package cook-and-serve vanilla pudding
1 (3 ounce) package cook-and-serve chocolate pudding
1 quart whole milk
4 (4 ounce) croissants
Powdered sugar

- Preheat oven to 325°. In large bowl, combine vanilla and chocolate pudding mixes with milk, whisking for 2 minutes or until they blend well.

- Cut croissants into 1-inch pieces and place in sprayed 3-quart baking dish. Spoon pudding mixture over croissant pieces and push pieces into liquid. Bake uncovered for 50 minutes or until bubbly around edges. Sprinkle powdered sugar over top of bread pudding. Cool 10 or 15 minutes before serving. Serves 6 to 10.

Fruit Crispy

6 cups peeled, sliced apples
3 tablespoons lemon juice
½ cup flour
⅓ cup oats
⅓ cup packed brown sugar
1 teaspoon cinnamon
¼ cup (½ stick) butter
⅓ cup chopped pecan

- Preheat oven to 425°. Toss apple slices with lemon juice and place in sprayed 7 x 11-inch baking dish.

- In bowl, combine flour, oats, brown sugar, cinnamon and a pinch of salt. Cut butter in with pastry blender and stir in pecans.

- Spoon mixture over apples and bake 25 to 30 minutes until fruit bubbles and topping begins to brown. Serves 4 to 6.

Make, Bake and Take

Delicious and "fancy" main dishes, favorite vegetable dishes, pleasing and practical breads, tasty pasta and splendid cakes and pies.

Chicken... 46
Beef... 84
Pork.. 98
Seafood 113
Breads 115
Vegetables 125
Side Dishes...................................... 145
Cakes... 162
Pies.. 165

Sassy Chicken
Over Tex-Mex Corn

2 teaspoons garlic powder
1 teaspoon ground cumin
⅔ cup flour
4 boneless, skinless chicken breast halves

- In shallow bowl, combine garlic powder, cumin, flour and an ample sprinkling of salt. Coat each side of chicken with flour mixture.

- Over medium-high heat, place small amount of oil in heavy skillet. Cut each chicken breast in half lengthwise. Brown each piece of chicken on both sides, reduce heat and add 2 tablespoons water to skillet. Cover and simmer for 15 minutes.

- Transfer chicken to foil-lined baking pan and warm at 250° until Tex-Mex Corn is ready to serve.

Tex-Mex Corn:
1 (10 ounce) can chicken broth
1½ cups hot salsa
1 (11 ounce) can Mexicorn®
1 cup instant rice

- Use same skillet, combine broth, salsa, corn and rice. Bring to a boil; reduce heat to low and simmer 10 minutes or until rice is tender.

- When ready to serve, spoon Tex-Mex Corn on platter and place chicken breasts over corn-rice mixture. Serves 4.

Stand firm in the Lord. Philippians 4:1

Supper-Ready Chicken

3 boneless, skinless chicken breasts, cooked
1 large onion, sliced
2 (15 ounce) cans new potatoes, drained, sliced
1 (10 ounce) can cream of celery soup
½ cup milk
1 cup shredded mozzarella cheese

- Preheat oven to 350°.
- Slice each chicken breast and place in sprayed 9 x 13-inch baking dish. Spread onion slices and potato slices over chicken.
- In saucepan, combine soup and milk and heat just until they mix well. Spoon over chicken-potato slices, cover and bake for 25 minutes. Remove from oven, sprinkle cheese over top and return to oven for 5 minutes. Serves 8.

 Sweet'n Spicy Chicken

1 pound boneless, skinless chicken breast halves
1 (1 ounce) packet taco seasoning
½ cup seasoned breadcrumbs
1 (16 ounce) jar chunky salsa
1½ cups peach preserves
2 cups cooked rice

- Cut chicken into ½-inch cubes and place in large, plastic bag. Add taco seasoning, breadcrumbs and toss to coat.
- In skillet, brown chicken in a little oil. Combine salsa and preserves, stir into skillet and bring mixture to a boil.
- Reduce heat, cover and simmer until juices run clear, about 15 minutes. Serve over hot, cooked rice. Serves 10.

Taco Chicken
Over Spanish Rice

1¼ cups flour
2 (1 ounce) packets taco seasoning
2 large eggs, beaten
8 boneless, skinless chicken breast halves
2 (15 ounce) cans Spanish rice
1 cup shredded Mexican 4-cheese blend

- Preheat oven to 350°.
- Place flour and taco seasoning in large shallow bowl.
- Place eggs and 3 tablespoons water in another shallow bowl and beat together.
- Dip each chicken breast in egg mixture, dredge in flour-taco mixture and press to apply ample amount of flour mixture.
- Place in sprayed 10 x 15-inch baking pan and arrange so chicken pieces do not touch. Bake for 55 to 60 minutes or until juices run clear.
- About 10 minutes before chicken is done, place Spanish rice in saucepan and stir in cheese. Stir constantly over medium meat, just until cheese melts.
- Spoon onto serving platter and place chicken pieces over hot rice. Serves 8.

Whoever does God's will is my brother and sister and mother. Mark 3:35

Spicy Orange Chicken
Over Noodles

1 pound boneless skinless chicken tenders
2 tablespoons oil
2 tablespoons soy sauce
1 (16 ounce) package frozen stir-fry vegetables, thawed
1 (6 ounce) package chow mein noodles

- In large skillet over medium-high heat, lightly brown chicken tenders in oil. Add soy sauce and stir-fry vegetables and cook about 8 minutes or until vegetables are tender-crisp.

Sauce:
⅔ cup orange marmalade
1 tablespoon olive oil
2 teaspoons lime juice
½ teaspoon dried ginger
¼ teaspoon cayenne pepper

- In saucepan, combine marmalade, oil, lime juice, ginger and cayenne pepper and mix well. Heat and pour over stir-fry chicken and vegetables and toss. Serve over chow mein noodles. Serves 10 to 12.

We love because he first loved us. First John 4:19

Rolled Chicken Florentine

6 boneless, skinless chicken breast halves
6 thin slices deli ham
6 thin slices Swiss cheese
1 (10 ounce) package frozen chopped spinach, thawed,
    drained
2 (10 ounce) cans cream of chicken soup
4 fresh green onions, finely chopped
1 (10 ounce) box chicken-flavored rice

- With flat side of meat mallet, pound chicken to ¼-inch thickness. Place ham slice, cheese slice and one-fourth cup well-drained spinach on each chicken piece and roll chicken from short end, jelly-roll style. Secure with wooden toothpicks.

- Place chicken in sprayed 9 x 13-inch glass baking dish. Cover with plastic wrap and microwave on HIGH for 4 minutes.

- Preheat oven to 325°.

- In bowl, stir together chicken soup, onions, ⅔ cup water and a little black pepper and mix well. Pour over chicken rolls, cover and bake for 25 minutes or until chicken is fork-tender.

- Cook rice according to package directions and place on serving platter. Spoon chicken and sauce over rice. Serves 6.

Love is patient, love is kind. First Corinthians 13:4

Pimento Cheese-Stuffed Fried Chicken

4 skinless, boneless chicken breast halves
½ cup milk
1 large egg, beaten
2 cups seasoned breadcrumbs
Oil
1 (16 ounce) carton pimento cheese

- Preheat oven to 350°.
- Dry chicken breasts with paper towels and sprinkle well with salt and pepper.
- Combine milk and beaten egg in shallow bowl and mix well. Place breadcrumbs in second shallow bowl. Dip chicken in milk mixture and dredge in breadcrumbs.
- In large skillet over medium-high heat, pour in oil to ⅛-inch depth and cook chicken about 10 to 12 minutes on each side. Transfer to baking sheet.
- Hold chicken with tongs and cut slit in 1 side of each chicken breast to form a pocket. Spoon about ¼ cup pimento cheese into each pocket and secure chicken pocket with toothpick. Bake about 3 minutes or until cheese melts. Serves 4.

Hold on to the good. 1 Thessalonians 5:21

Orange Chicken Over Rice

2 pounds boneless, skinless chicken thighs
2 bell peppers, seeded, cut in strips
1 (1 ounce) packet dry onion soup mix
1 (6 ounce) can frozen orange juice concentrate, thawed
1 (6 ounce) box long grain and wild rice mix

- Preheat oven to 350°.
- In large skillet, brown chicken in a little oil and place in sprayed 9 x 13-inch baking pan. Place bell pepper strips over chicken.
- In bowl, combine dry onion soup mix, orange juice concentrate and 1½ cups water and mix well. Pour over chicken, cover and bake for 50 minutes.
- Prepare rice mix according to package directions and place on serving plate. Spoon chicken mixture over rice and serve hot. Serves 10 to 12.

Imperial Chicken Casserole

5 boneless, skinless chicken breast halves, cooked, cubed
1 (1 pint) carton sour cream
1 (7 ounce) package ready-cut spaghetti
2 (10 ounce) cans cream of chicken soup
1 (4 ounce) can mushrooms, drained
½ cup (1 stick) butter, melted
1 cup fresh, grated parmesan cheese

- Preheat oven to 325°.
- Combine chicken, sour cream, spaghetti, chicken soup, mushrooms and butter in bowl.
- Pour into sprayed 9 x 13-inch baking dish, cover and bake for 50 minutes. Remove from oven and sprinkle cheese on top of casserole. Return to oven for 5 minutes. Serves 5.

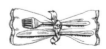 Crunchy Baked Chicken

¼ pound (1 stick) butter, melted
2 tablespoons mayonnaise
2 tablespoons white wine Worcestershire sauce
1 (6 ounce) can french-fried onions, crushed
6 boneless, skinless chicken breasts halves

- Preheat oven to 350°.
- In shallow bowl, combine melted butter, mayonnaise and Worcestershire sauce. Place crushed onions in another shallow bowl.
- Dry chicken breasts with paper towels; dip first into butter mixture and dredge each chicken breast in crushed onions. Place in large baking pan and arrange so pieces do not touch.
- Bake for 30 minutes or until chicken juices run clear. Serves 6.

Glazed Chicken Over Rice

4 boneless, skinless chicken breast halves, cubed
1 (20 ounce) can pineapple chunks with juice
½ cup honey-mustard grill-and-glaze sauce
1 red bell pepper, seeded, chopped
1 cup instant white rice, cooked

- Place a little oil in skillet and brown chicken. Reduce heat to medium and cook 15 minutes. Add pineapple, honey-mustard sauce and bell pepper and bring to a boil.
- Reduce heat to low and simmer 15 minutes or until sauce thickens slightly. Serve over hot, cooked rice. Serves 4.

Marinated Salsa Chicken

Chicken:
6 boneless, skinless chicken breast halves
1 tablespoon cornstarch

Marinade:
1 (16 ounce) jar salsa
¾ cup honey
½ cup light soy sauce
2 tablespoons oil
½ teaspoon dried ginger

- Dry each chicken piece with paper towels. In bowl, combine all marinade ingredients and mix well.
- Pour 1½ cups into sealable plastic bag, add chicken and refrigerate 2 to 3 hours. Cover and refrigerate remaining marinade.
- Preheat oven to 350°.
- Drain chicken, discard marinade and place chicken in sprayed 9 x 13-inch baking dish. Top with remaining refrigerated marinade and bake, uncovered, for 25 to 30 minutes or until juices run clear.
- Remove chicken and keep warm. In small saucepan, combine cornstarch with 2 tablespoons water and stir in pan juices.
- Bring to a boil and cook about 2 minutes, stirring constantly, until it thickens. Pour sauce over chicken to serve. Serves 6.

Lord, teach us to pray. Luke 11:1

Honey-Glazed Chicken

¾ cup flour
½ teaspoon cayenne pepper
1 broiler-fryer chicken, quartered
¼ cup (½ stick) butter, divided
⅓ cup packed brown sugar
⅓ cup honey
⅓ cup lemon juice
1 tablespoon light soy sauce

- Preheat oven to 350°.

- In shallow bowl, combine flour, cayenne pepper and ½ teaspoon salt. Dredge chicken quarters (cut wing tips off) in flour mixture.

- Place 2 tablespoons butter in large, heavy skillet and brown chicken over high heat on both sides. Transfer to sprayed 9 x 13-inch baking dish.

- In same skillet, place remaining butter, brown sugar, honey, lemon juice and soy sauce and bring to a boil.

- Remove from heat and pour mixture over chicken quarters. Bake, uncovered for 35 to 40 minutes; baste several times with pan drippings. Serves 4 to 6.

Above all else, guard your heart, for it is the wellspring of life. Proverbs 4:23

Chicken and Potatoes

5 boneless, skinless chicken breast halves
5 slices onion
5 new, red potatoes, quartered
1 (10 ounce) can cream of celery soup
1 (10 ounce) can cream of chicken soup

- Preheat oven to 325°.
- Place chicken breasts in sprayed 9 x 13-inch baking dish. Top chicken with onion slices and place potatoes around chicken.
- Combine both soups and ½ cup water and heat slightly. Pour mixture over chicken and vegetables.
- Cover and bake for 1 hour. Serves 5.

Encore Chicken

6 boneless, skinless chicken breast halves
1 (16 ounce) jar hot, thick-and-chunky salsa
1½ cups packed light brown sugar
1 tablespoon dijon-style mustard
Hot cooked instant brown rice

- Preheat oven to 325°.
- In large skillet with a little oil, brown chicken breasts and place in sprayed 9 x 13-inch baking dish.
- Combine salsa, brown sugar, mustard and ½ teaspoon salt and pour over chicken. Cover and bake for 45 minutes. Serve over hot, cooked brown rice. Serves 6.

For everyone who exalts himself will be humbled. Luke 14:11

Mushrooms, Noodles and Chicken

½ cup (1 stick) butter
1 green and 1 red bell pepper, seeded, chopped
½ cup flour
1½ teaspoons seasoned salt
1½ cups milk
1 (14 ounce) can beef broth
1 (10 ounce) can cream of mushroom soup
1 (12 ounce) package medium egg noodles, cooked, drained
3 - 4 cups cooked, cubed chicken
1 (8 ounce) package shredded cheddar cheese

- Preheat oven to 350º.

- On medium-high heat, melt butter in large skillet. Cook and stir bell peppers for 10 minutes. Stir in flour and seasoned salt and mix well.

- While still on medium-high heat, slowly stir in milk, beef broth and 1 teaspoon pepper. Cook until mixture is thick and pour into large bowl.

- Fold in mushroom soup, noodles and chicken and transfer to sprayed 11 x 15-inch baking pan. Cover and bake 35 minutes or until thoroughly hot. Uncover, sprinkle cheese over casserole and return to oven for additional 5 minutes. Serves 12.

Neither height nor depth nor anything else in all creation will be able to separate us from the love of God. Romans 8:39

Creamy Tarragon Chicken

1½ cups flour
6 boneless, skinless chicken breast halves
2 tablespoons oil
1 (10 ounce) can chicken broth
1 cup milk
2 teaspoons dried tarragon
1 (4 ounce) can sliced mushrooms, drained
2 (8 ounce) packages microwave roasted chicken-flavored rice

- Mix flour and a little salt and pepper on wax paper, coat chicken and save extra flour. Heat oil in large skillet over medium-high heat and cook chicken breasts, turning once, about 10 minutes or until light brown. Transfer to plate.

- In same skillet, stir in 2 tablespoons flour-salt mixture. Whisk in chicken broth, milk and tarragon, heat and stir constantly until it bubbles.

- Add mushrooms and return chicken to skillet. Cover and simmer for 10 to 15 minutes or until sauce thickens.

- Microwave rice according to package directions and place on serving platter. Spoon chicken and sauce over rice. Serves 6.

He who pursues righteousness and love finds life, prosperity and honor.
Proverbs 21:21

Green Chile-Chicken Casserole

1 green bell pepper, seeded, chopped
3 ribs celery, chopped
¾ cup chopped green onions
½ cup (1 stick) butter
1 (7 ounce) can chopped green chilies
1½ cups rice
1 (8 ounce) carton sour cream
3 boneless, skinless chicken breast halves, cooked, sliced
1 (14 ounce) can chicken broth

- Preheat oven to 325°.
- Combine bell pepper, celery and green onions in skillet with butter and saute 5 minutes. Transfer to mixing bowl.
- Stir in green chilies, rice, sour cream, chicken, chicken broth, ¼ cup water and a little salt and pepper. Pour into sprayed 9 x 13-inch baking dish.
- Cover and bake for 40 minutes, uncover and continue to bake for 10 minutes. Serves 6 to 8.

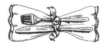

You cannot understand the work of God, the Maker of all things.
Ecclesiastes 11:5

Chicken a la Orange

1 (11 ounce) can mandarin oranges, drained
1 (6 ounce) can frozen orange juice concentrate
1 tablespoon lemon juice
1 tablespoon cornstarch
6 boneless, skinless chicken breast halves
2 tablespoons garlic-and-herb seasoning
2 tablespoons butter

- In saucepan, combine oranges, orange juice concentrate, lemon juice, ⅔ cup water and cornstarch. Stir constantly over medium heat until mixture thickens. Set aside.

- Sprinkle chicken breasts with herb seasoning and place in skillet with butter. Cook about 7 minutes on each side until brown.

- Lower heat and spoon orange juice mixture over chicken, cover and simmer about 20 minutes. Add a little water if sauce gets too thick.

- Serve over hot, cooked rice. Serves 6.

Rich and poor have this in common: The Lord is the Maker of them all.
Proverbs 22:2

Cheesy Chicken Pie

1 (12 ounce) package shredded cheddar cheese, divided
1 (10 ounce) package frozen peas and carrots, thawed
1 red bell pepper, seeded, chopped
2 cups cooked, diced chicken breasts
1½ cups half-and-half cream
3 large eggs, beaten
¾ cup baking mix

- Preheat oven to 350°.

- In large bowl, combine 2 cups cheese, peas and carrots, bell pepper and chicken. Spread into sprayed 10-inch deep-dish pie plate.

- In mixing bowl, combine cream, eggs, baking mix and a little salt and pepper and mix well. Spoon mixture over cheese-vegetable mixture, but do not stir.

- Cover and bake for 35 minutes or until center of pie is firm. Remove from oven, sprinkle remaining cheese over top and return to oven for 5 minutes. Serves 8.

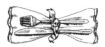

For God so loved the world, that he gave his only begotten Son. John 3:16

Cashew Chicken and Veggies

1 pound boneless, skinless chicken breast halves
2 tablespoons cornstarch
1 tablespoon soy sauce
1 teaspoon grated fresh ginger
1 (16 ounce) package frozen broccoli florets, thawed
1 (10 ounce) package frozen green peas, thawed
1 (1 ounce) packet savory herb-garlic soup mix
⅔ cup whole cashews
1 (6 ounce) package chicken and herb-flavored rice, cooked

- Cut chicken crosswise into ¼-inch wide strips. In medium bowl, combine cornstarch, soy sauce and ginger and mix well. Add chicken strips and stir to coat well.

- In large skillet with a little oil, stir-fry broccoli and peas for 3 minutes and remove to warm plate.

- In same skillet with a little oil, stir-fry chicken until all pieces change color. Stir in ½ cup water and soup mix.

- Cook on medium heat about 5 minutes until soup mix coats chicken well.

- Return cooked vegetables to skillet, add cashews and cook until thoroughly hot. Serve chicken and vegetables over hot, cooked rice. Serves 12.

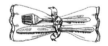

Turn from evil and do good; seek peace and pursue it. Psalm 34:14

Almond-Crusted Chicken

1 egg
¼ cup seasoned breadcrumbs
1 cup sliced almonds
4 boneless, skinless chicken breast halves
1 (5 ounce) package grated parmesan cheese

- Preheat oven to 350°.

- Place egg and 1 tablespoon water in shallow bowl and beat. In another shallow bowl, combine breadcrumbs and almonds.

- Dip each chicken breast in egg, then in almond mixture and place in sprayed 9 x 13-inch baking pan.

- Bake uncovered for 20 minutes. Remove chicken from oven and sprinkle parmesan cheese over each breast and cook another 15 minutes or until almonds and cheese are golden brown.

Sauce:

1 teaspoon minced garlic
⅓ cup finely chopped onion
2 tablespoons oil
1 cup white wine
¼ cup teriyaki sauce

- In saucepan, saute garlic and onion in oil. Add wine and teriyaki sauce, bring to a boil and reduce heat. Simmer about 10 minutes or until mixture reduces by half. Serve sauce over chicken. Serves 4.

Great is the Lord and most worthy of praise. Psalm 48:1

Chicken-Taco Pie

1 pound boneless, skinless chicken breast halves
1 (1 ounce) packet taco seasoning mix
1 green and 1 red bell pepper, seeded, finely chopped
1 (8 ounce) package shredded Mexican 4-cheese blend
1 (8 ounce) package corn muffin mix
1 egg
⅓ cup milk

- Preheat oven to 400°.

- Cut chicken into 1-inch chunks and cook on medium-high heat in large skillet with a little oil. Cook about 10 minutes and drain.

- Stir in taco seasoning, bell peppers and ¾ cup water. Reduce heat, cook another 10 minutes and stir several times. Spoon into sprayed 9-inch deep-dish pan and sprinkle with cheese.

- Prepare corn muffin mix with egg and milk and mix well. Spoon over top of pie and bake for 20 minutes or until top is golden brown. Let stand about 5 minutes before serving. Serves 8 to 10.

For God so loved the world that he gave his only begotten Son. John 3:16

Chicken Linguine

1 pound boneless, skinless chicken breast halves, cut into strips
Oil
1 (28 ounce) can garlic-onion spaghetti sauce
1 (16 ounce) package frozen broccoli, carrots and cauliflower,
  thawed
1 bell pepper, seeded, chopped
⅓ cup grated parmesan cheese
1 (12 ounce) package dry linguine

- In large skillet over medium heat, cook half chicken strips in a little oil until light brown. Remove and set aside. Repeat with remaining chicken and set aside.

- In same skillet combine spaghetti sauce, vegetables and cheese and bring to a boil. Reduce heat to medium-low, cover and cook 10 minutes or until vegetables are tender. Stir occasionally.

- Return chicken to skillet and heat thoroughly. Cook linguine according to package directions and drain.

- Place cooked linguine on serving platter and spoon chicken mixture over linguine. Serves 12.

TIP: Break linguine into thirds before cooking to make serving a little easier.

Make, Bake & Take: Chicken

It is more blessed to give than to receive. Acts 20:35

Party Chicken

1 large chicken, quartered
1 (8 ounce) bottle Russian dressing
1 (12 ounce) bottle apricot preserves
1 (1 ounce) packet dry onion soup mix
1 (8 ounce) can pineapple rings, drained
1 bell pepper, seeded, cut into rings

- Preheat oven to 350°.
- Arrange chicken pieces in sprayed 9 x 13-inch baking dish.
- In large bowl, combine dressing, preserves, soup mix, ¼ cup water and a little pepper. Stir well to mix and pour over chicken pieces. (Scrape sides of bowl to get all bits of soup mix and preserves.)
- Cover and bake for 1 hour. Remove from oven, place pineapple and bell pepper rings over chicken and cook for another 15 minutes. Serves 4 to 6.

Spaghetti Toss

1 (10 ounce) package thin spaghetti
1 (10 ounce) package frozen sugar snap peas
2 tablespoons butter
3 cups rotisserie cooked chicken strips
1 (11 ounce) can mandarin oranges, drained
⅔ cup stir-fry sauce

- Cook spaghetti according to package directions; stir in sugar snap peas and cook 1 additional minute. Drain and stir in butter. Spoon into serving bowl.
- Add chicken, oranges and stir-fry sauce and toss to coat. Serves 10.

Alfredo-Chicken Spaghetti

1 (8 ounce) package thin spaghetti, broken in thirds
2 teaspoons minced garlic
1 (16 ounce) jar alfredo sauce
About ¼ cup milk
1 (10 ounce) box broccoli florets, thawed
2 cups cooked, diced chicken
1 cup shredded mozzarella cheese

- Preheat oven to 350°.
- Cook spaghetti according to package directions and drain. Place back in saucepan and stir in garlic, alfredo sauce and milk; mix well.
- Add drained broccoli florets and cook on medium heat, about 5 minutes, stirring several times or until broccoli is tender; add more milk if needed.
- Stir in diced chicken and spoon into sprayed 7 x 11-inch baking dish. Cover and bake for 20 minutes.
- Remove from oven and sprinkle cheese over top. Return to oven for additional 5 minutes. Serves 8.

A good name is more desirable than great riches; to be esteemed is better than silver and gold. Proverbs 22:1

Supreme Chicken and Green Beans

1 (16 ounce) package seasoning blend onions and bell peppers
3 cups cooked, diced chicken
1 (6 ounce) package long grain and wild rice, cooked
1 (10 ounce) can cream of chicken soup
1 (4 ounce) can chopped pimentos
1 (15 ounce) can French-style green beans, drained
½ cup slivered almonds
1 cup mayonnaise
3 cups lightly crushed potato chips

- Preheat oven to 350°.
- In skillet with a little oil, saute onions and bell peppers.
- In large bowl, combine onions and bell peppers, chicken, rice, chicken soup, pimentos, green beans, almonds, mayonnaise and a little salt and pepper. Mix well.
- Spray deep 9 x 13-inch baking dish and spoon mixture into dish.
- Sprinkle crushed potato chips over casserole and bake for 35 minutes or until chips are light brown. Serves 10 to 12.

Where there is no vision, the people perish. Proverbs 29:18

Ranch Chicken To Go

1 (8 ounce) package favorite pasta
½ cup (1 stick) butter, melted
1 (10 ounce) can cream of chicken soup
1 (1 ounce) packet ranch salad dressing mix
2 (15 ounce) cans peas and carrots, drained
3 cups cooked, cubed chicken
1 (2.8 ounce) can french-fried onion rings

- Preheat oven to 325°.

- Cook pasta according to package directions.

- In saucepan, combine butter, soup, dressing mix, peas and carrots. Stir occasionally over medium heat until all ingredients mix well and are thoroughly hot. Toss with cooked pasta and chicken and spoon into sprayed 3-quart baking dish. Cover and bake for 15 minutes.

- Remove from oven, sprinkle onion rings over top and return to oven for another 15 minutes. Serves 10 to 12.

Quick Chicken Supper

1 (16 ounce) package frozen broccoli florets, thawed
1 (10 ounce) can cream of chicken soup
⅔ cup mayonnaise
1 cup shredded cheddar cheese
3 cups cooked, cubed chicken
2 cups crushed cheese crackers

- Preheat oven to 350°.

- In large bowl, combine broccoli, soup, mayonnaise, cheese and chicken and mix well. Pour into sprayed 3-quart baking dish, cover and bake for 20 minutes.

- Uncover, sprinkle cheese crackers over top of casserole and return to oven for additional 20 minutes. Serves 10 to 12.

Confetti Squash and Chicken

1 pound yellow squash, sliced
1 pound zucchini, sliced
2 cups cooked, cubed chicken
1 (10 ounce) can cream of chicken soup
1 (8 ounce) carton sour cream
1 (4 ounce) can chopped pimento, drained
½ cup (1 stick) butter, melted
1 (6 ounce) box herb stuffing mix

- Preheat oven to 350°.
- In large saucepan, cook squash and zucchini in salted water about 10 minutes. Drain, stir in chicken, soup, sour cream and pimentos and mix well.
- Combine melted butter and stuffing mix, add to vegetable-chicken mixture and mix well. Spoon into sprayed 9 x 13-inch baking dish. Cover and bake for 35 minutes. Serves 10.

You know that the testing of your faith develops perseverance.
James 1:3

Chop Suey Veggies and Chicken

3 cups cooked, cubed chicken
2 (10 ounce) cans cream of chicken soup
2 (15 ounce) cans chop suey vegetables, drained
1 (8 ounce) can sliced water chestnuts, drained
1 (16 ounce) package frozen seasoning blend onions and bell peppers
½ teaspoon hot sauce
½ - 1 teaspoon curry powder
2 cups chow mein noodles

- Preheat oven to 350°.
- In large bowl, combine chicken, soup, vegetables, water chestnuts, onions and bell peppers, hot sauce, curry powder and a little salt and pepper and mix well.
- Spoon into sprayed 9 x 13-inch baking dish. Sprinkle chow mein noodles over top and bake for 40 minutes. Serves 10 to 12.

Always giving thanks to God the Father for everything, in the name of our Lord Jesus Christ. Ephesians 5:20

Chicken-Green Bean Bake

2 cups instant rice
1 (16 ounce) package shredded Velveeta® cheese
1 (16 ounce) package frozen cut green beans, thawed
3 cups cooked, cubed chicken
2 cups coarsely crushed potato chips

- Preheat oven to 325°.
- Cook rice in large saucepan according to package directions and stir in cheese and extra ¼ cup water. Stir and mix until cheese melts.
- Cook green beans according to package directions and drain. Stir in rice-cheese mixture, add cubed chicken and mix well. Spoon into sprayed 9 x 13-inch baking dish. Top with crushed potato chips and bake for 20 minutes or until chips are light brown. Serves 10.

Barbecue Chicken Salad

¼ cup barbecue sauce
2 tablespoons cider vinegar
3 tablespoons olive oil
1 (9 ounce) package romaine lettuce, cut in 1-inch pieces
2 cups skinless rotisserie chicken meat
1 (11 ounce) can Mexicorn®, drained
1 (15 ounce) can black beans, rinsed, drained
1 (4 ounce) can chopped green chilies

- In small bowl, mix barbecue sauce, vinegar and 1 tablespoon water with wire whisk. Pour oil in slow, steady stream and whisk while pouring in oil.
- In large deep salad bowl, toss romaine with ¼ cup dressing. Arrange chicken, corn and beans on top of romaine. Sprinkle with chilies and drizzle remaining dressing. Toss just before serving. Serves 8.

Chicken Squares

2 (12 ounce) cans chicken breast chunks with liquid
1 (8 ounce) carton cream cheese, softened
¼ cup finely chopped onion
2 tablespoons sesame seeds
1 (8 count) package refrigerated crescent rolls

- Preheat oven to 350°.
- Pour chicken with liquid in mixing bowl. Add cream cheese and beat until creamy. Add onion, sesame seeds and a little salt and pepper. Mix well.
- Open package of crescent rolls, but do not divide into triangles. Form 4 squares using 2 triangles for each. Pinch seam in middle of each square together and pat into larger square.
- Spoon about ½ cup chicken mixture into center of each square. Fold corners up into center and lay like flower petals so roll seals. Repeat for all squares.
- Place each roll on sprayed baking sheet and bake about 15 minutes or until golden brown. Serves 4.

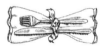

And forgive us our debts, as we forgive our debtors. Matthew 6:12

Chicken-Spaghetti Bake

1 (12 ounce) package spaghetti
1 (16 ounce) package frozen seasoning blend onion and bell peppers
3 ribs celery, sliced
1 (15 ounce) can Mexican stewed tomatoes
1 (10 ounce) can chicken broth
4 cups cooked, cubed chicken
1 (12 ounce) package shredded Velveeta® cheese

- Preheat oven to 350°.
- Cook spaghetti according to package directions and drain.
- In large saucepan with a little oil, saute onion, bell peppers and celery. Add tomatoes, broth, chicken and a little salt and pepper. Stir in half cheese and spoon into sprayed 9 x 13-inch baking dish.
- Cover and bake for 40 minutes. Remove from oven and sprinkle remaining cheese over top of casserole. Return to oven for 5 minutes. Serves 12.

A man's steps are directed by the Lord. Proverbs 20:24

Chicken Couscous

1¼ cups chicken broth
1 (5.6 ounce) package toasted pine nut couscous, cooked
1 rotisserie chicken, boned, cubed
1 (4 ounce) can chopped pimento
½ cup feta cheese
1 (16 ounce) package frozen green peas
1 tablespoon dried basil
1 tablespoon lemon juice

- Heat broth and seasoning packet from couscous in microwave on HIGH for 4 minutes or until broth begins to boil. Place couscous in large bowl and stir in broth. Cover and let stand for 5 minutes.
- Fluff couscous with fork and add chicken, pimento, cheese, peas, basil and lemon juice. Toss to blend well. Serve warm. Serves 10.

TIP: Couscous is a quick alternative to rice or pasta and it couldn't be easier to make. All you have to do is add boiling water (or in this case, broth).

For the Lord God is a sun and a shield. Psalm 84:11

Chicken Lasagna

1 (16 ounce) jar alfredo sauce
1 (4 ounce) can diced pimentos, drained
⅓ cup cooking white wine
1 (10 ounce) box frozen chopped spinach, thawed
1 (15 ounce) carton ricotta cheese
½ cup grated parmesan cheese
1 egg, beaten
8 lasagna noodles
3 cups cooked, shredded chicken
1 (12 ounce) package shredded cheddar cheese

- Preheat oven to 350°.
- In large bowl, combine alfredo sauce, pimentos and wine; reserve ½ cup for top of lasagna.
- Drain spinach well, place in separate bowl and add ricotta, parmesan cheese and egg. Mix well.
- Spray deep 9 x 13-inch baking dish and place 4 noodles in dish. Layer with half remaining sauce, half spinach-ricotta mixture and half chicken. (Spinach-ricotta mixture will be fairly dry so you will need to "spoon" it on and spread out.)
- Sprinkle with half cheese. For last layer, place noodles, remaining sauce, remaining spinach-rocotta mixture, reamaining chicken and reserved sauce on top.
- Cover and bake for 45 minutes. Sprinkle remaining cheese and return to oven, uncovered for 6 minutes. Let casserole stand 10 minutes before serving. Serves 10 to 12.

Blessed are the poor in spirit, for theirs is the kingdom of heaven.
Matthew 5:3

Chicken-Sausage Casserole

1 pound pork sausage
1 (1 pound) carton fresh mushrooms, sliced
2 sweet red bell peppers, seeded, chopped
3 cups cooked, cubed chicken
1 (6 ounce) box long grain and wild rice mix, cooked
1 (10 ounce) can cream of chicken soup
1 (10 ounce) can chicken broth
2 cups buttery cracker crumbs

- Preheat oven to 350°.
- In large skillet, brown and cook sausage and drain. Add mushrooms and bell peppers and saute 5 minutes. Stir in chicken and mix well.
- Cook rice according to package directions.
- In large saucepan, combine chicken soup, chicken broth and cooked rice. Stir in sausage-chicken mixture and gently mix to blend well.
- Spoon into sprayed 9 x 13-inch baking dish. Sprinkle buttery crumbs over top and bake for 30 minutes. Serves 10 to 12.

For to me, to live is Christ and to die is gain. Philippians 1:21

Baked Chicken and Mushrooms

2 (10 ounce) cans cream of mushroom soup
1 soup can milk
2 teaspoons curry powder
1 (4 ounce) can sliced mushrooms, drained
2½ cups cooked instant rice
1 (8 ounce) can green peas, drained
3 cups cooked, cubed chicken
2 cups slightly crushed potato chips

- Preheat oven to 350°.
- In large bowl, combine soup, milk, curry powder, mush-rooms, rice, peas, chicken and a little salt and pepper and mix well.
- Spoon into sprayed 9 x 13-inch baking pan. Cover and bake for 20 minutes.
- Remove from oven, sprinkle with crushed potato chips and return to oven for another 20 minutes. Serves 10.

Chicken and Stuffing Bake

2 (6 ounce) packages herb-seasoned stuffing
1 (16 ounce) can whole berry cranberry sauce
1 cup chopped pecans
2 (12 ounce) cans chunk white chicken
2 (10 ounce) cans chicken gravy

- Preheat oven to 375°.
- In large saucepan, prepare stuffing according to package directions. Stir in cranberry sauce and pecans and set aside.
- In sprayed 9 x 13-inch baking dish, arrange layer of chicken and pour gravy over chicken.
- Spoon stuffing mixture evenly over all and bake un-covered for 15 to 20 minutes or until hot and bubbly. Serves 8.

Chicken-Broccoli Bake

1 (10 ounce) can cream of chicken soup
⅔ cup milk
2 cups cubed rotisserie chicken
1 (16 ounce) package broccoli florets, thawed
1 (4 ounce) can chopped pimentos, drained
1 (7.7 ounce) pouch cheese-garlic biscuit mix
1 teaspoon dried parsley

- Preheat oven to 400°.

- Combine soup and milk in large bowl and blend well. Stir in chicken, broccoli and pimentos. Spoon into sprayed 3-quart round baking dish and bake for 20 minutes.

- About 5 minutes before removing dish from oven, prepare biscuit mix according to package directions and use ½ cup water and dried parsley.

- Drop 8 large spoonfuls of dough around edges of casserole onto chicken mixture.

- Continue baking for 15 minutes or until bubbly and biscuits are golden brown. Serves 8.

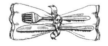

For in the same way you judge others, you will be judged, and with the measure you use, it will be measured to you. John 7:2

Make, Bake & Take: Chicken

Chicken on the Ranch

¼ cup flour
1 (1 ounce) packet ranch salad dressing mix
6 boneless, skinless chicken breast halves
Oil
1 (16 ounce) jar salsa
¾ cup packed brown sugar
1 tablespoon mustard
Hot cooked rice

- Preheat oven to 350º.
- Combine flour and salad dressing mix in shallow bowl. Dredge each chicken breast in flour mixture.
- Place a little oil in large skillet and brown 3 pieces of chicken at a time. Transfer chicken to sprayed 9 x 13-inch baking pan.
- In small bowl, combine salsa, brown sugar and mustard and mix well. Pour over chicken. Cover and bake 30 minutes, remove cover and continue baking additional 20 minutes. Serve over hot, cooked rice. Serves 6.

I served the Lord with great humility and with tears. Acts 20:19

Turkey-Stuffing Casserole

3 - 4 cups cooked, chopped turkey
1 (16 ounce) package frozen broccoli florets, thawed
1 (10 ounce) can cream of chicken soup
⅔ cup sour cream
1 (8 ounce) package shredded Swiss cheese
1 (6 ounce) package turkey stuffing mix
½ cup chopped walnuts

- Preheat oven to 325°.
- Spread chopped turkey in 9 x 13-inch baking dish and top with broccoli florets.
- In bowl, combine soup, sour cream and cheese and spread over broccoli. In another bowl, combine stuffing mix, walnuts and ¾ cup water and spread evenly over broccoli. Bake for 40 minutes or until hot and bubbly. Serves 12.

Turkey and Rice Supper

¾ pound cooked, sliced turkey
2 cups cooked instant brown rice
1 (10 ounce) can cream of chicken soup
1 (10 ounce) can chopped tomatoes and green chilies
1½ cups crushed tortilla chips

- Preheat oven to 350°.
- Place turkey slices in bottom of sprayed 7 x 11-inch baking dish.
- In bowl, combine rice, chicken soup and tomatoes and green chilies, mix well. Spoon mixture over turkey slices. Sprinkle crushed tortilla chips over top of casserole and bake, uncovered for 40 minutes. Serves 8.

Cranberry-Turkey and Stuffing

1 (6 ounce) package herb-seasoned chicken stuffing
2 tablespoons butter
1 onion, chopped
2 ribs celery, sliced
1 cup whole cranberry sauce
1 pound thick-sliced deli turkey
1 (12 ounce) can turkey gravy

- Preheat oven to 350°.

- Prepare stuffing mix according to package directions.
  In skillet, melt butter and saute onion and celery. Add
  onion, celery and cranberry sauce to stuffing mixture and
  mix well.

- Place turkey slices in sprayed 9 x 13-inch baking pan
  and pour gravy over turkey. Spoon stuffing-cranberry
  mixture over turkey and gravy. Bake for 20 minutes or
  until casserole is hot and bubbly. Serves 10 to 12.

Turkey and Noodles Plus

1 (12 ounce) package medium egg noodles
3 cups cooked, diced turkey
1 (16 ounce) package frozen peas and carrots, thawed
2 (12 ounce) jars turkey gravy
2 cups slightly crushed potato chips

- Preheat oven to 350°.

- Cook noodles according to package directions and
  drain. Arrange alternate layers of noodles, turkey, peas,
  carrots and gravy in sprayed 9 x 13-inch baking dish.
  Cover and bake for 20 minutes.

- Remove from oven, sprinkle potato chips over casserole
  and return to oven for 15 minutes or until chips are light
  brown. Serves 12.

Baked Turkey and Dressing

1 (6 ounce) package turkey stuffing
3 cups cooked, diced turkey
1 sweet red bell pepper, seeded, chopped
2 tablespoons dried parsley flakes
1 (10 ounce) can cream of chicken soup
1 (8 ounce) carton sour cream
¼ cup (½ stick) butter, melted
1 teaspoon ground cumin
1½ cups shredded mozzarella cheese

- Preheat oven to 350°.
- In large mixing bowl, combine all ingredients except mozzarella cheese. Mix well and spoon into sprayed 9 x 13-inch baking dish.
- Cover and bake for 35 minutes. Uncover, sprinkle with cheese and bake and additional 5 minutes. Serves 10 to 12.

The heavens declare the glory of God; the skies proclaim the work of his hands. Psalm 19:1

Beef Patties in Onion Sauce

2½ pounds lean ground beef
1 (1 ounce) packet savory herb-garlic soup mix
1 egg, beaten
2 (10 ounce) cans French onion soup

- Preheat oven to 350°.
- Combine beef, soup mix, egg and ¼ cup water and shape into patties about ¾-inch thick. Brown on both sides in large skillet over high heat.
- Place patties in sprayed 9 x 13-inch baking pan and pour onion soup and ¾ cup water over patties. Cover and bake for 35 minutes. Serves 8.

Beefy-Rice Casserole

1 pound lean ground beef
¾ cup white rice
1 (10 ounce) package frozen corn, thawed
1 (10 ounce) can French onion soup
1 (2.8 ounce) can french-fried onion rings

- Preheat oven to 325°.
- Brown ground beef, drain and place in sprayed 3-quart baking dish.
- Stir in rice, corn, onion soup and ½ cup water. Cover and bake for 30 minutes. Uncover and sprinkle onion rings over top of casserole and return to oven for 15 minutes. Serves 5 to 6.

Whatsoever thy hand findeth to do, do it with thy might. Ecclesiastes 9:10

Beef-Potato Casserole

1½ pounds lean ground beef
1 (15 ounce) can sloppy Joe sauce
1 (10 ounce) can beef broth
1 (20 ounce) package frozen hash brown potatoes, thawed
1 (8 ounce) package shredded cheddar cheese

- Preheat oven to 375°.
- In skillet, cook beef over medium heat until no longer pink and stir to crumble. Add sloppy Joe sauce, beef broth and a little black pepper.
- Place hash browns in sprayed 9 x 13-inch baking dish and top with beef-broth mixture.
- Cover and bake for 30 minutes. Uncover, sprinkle cheese over top and continue baking for additional 5 minutes. Serves 8.

Meatloaf Tonight

1½ pounds lean ground beef
1 (10 ounce) can golden cream of mushroom soup
1 (10 ounce) can cream of celery soup
1 (1 ounce) packet savory herb-garlic soup mix
1 cup cooked instant rice

- Preheat oven to 350°.
- Combine ground beef, both soups, dry onion soup mix and cooked rice. Place on sprayed 9 x 13-inch baking pan and form into loaf.
- Bake for 45 to 50 minutes or until loaf is golden brown. Serves 8.

Everything is possible for him who believes. Mark 9:23

Black Bean Chili Casserole

1 pound lean ground beef
1 onion, finely chopped
2 (15 ounce) cans black beans, drained
1 teaspoon cumin
1 teaspoon chili powder
1½ cups thick-and-chunky salsa
1 (6.5 ounce) package corn muffin mix
1 egg
¼ cup milk

- Preheat oven to 375°.
- In large skillet with a little oil, cook beef and onion on medium-high heat for 8 to 10 minutes. Stir in black beans (or pinto beans if you prefer), cumin, chili powder, salsa and a little salt. Bring to a boil and reduce heat to medium. Cook 5 minutes and stir occasionally. Spoon into sprayed 3-quart round baking dish.
- In small bowl, prepare muffin mix according to package directions with egg and milk.
- Drop 8 spoonfuls batter around edge of baking dish, onto bean-beef mixture. Bake uncovered for 20 to 25 minutes or until topping is golden brown. Serves 6 to 8.

Ye shall know the truth and the truth shall make you free. John 8:32

Creamy Beef Casserole

1½ pounds lean ground beef
1 onion, chopped
1 green bell pepper, seeded, chopped
1 (15 ounce) can tomato sauce
1 (7 ounce) can chopped green chilies
1 (12 ounce) package medium noodles
1 (16 ounce) carton small curd cottage cheese
¾ cup mayonnaise
1 cup shredded 4-cheese blend

- Preheat oven to 350°.

- In large skillet over medium-high heat, brown beef, onion and bell pepper. Stir in tomato sauce, green chilies and a little salt and pepper. Reduce heat, stir well and simmer 20 minutes.

- Cook noodles according to package directions and drain well.

- In bowl, combine cottage cheese and mayonnaise and fold into noodles. Spoon noodle mixture into sprayed 9 x 13-inch baking dish.

- Pour beef mixture over noodle mixture. Cover and bake 30 minutes. Remove cover, sprinkle cheese on top and return to oven for additional 5 minutes. Serves 6.

That you love one another as I have loved you. John 13:35

Good Night Casserole Supper

1 pound lean ground beef
1 onion, chopped
1 red and 1 green pepper, seeded, chopped
2 (10 ounce) cans golden cream of mushroom soup
⅔ cup white rice
4 tablespoons soy sauce
1 (2.8 ounce) can french-fried onion rings

- Preheat oven to 350°.
- Brown ground beef and onions in large skillet and drain off fat. Pour into sprayed 9 x 13-inch baking dish.
- Stir in bell peppers, both cans soup, rice, soy sauce, ¾ cup water and a little salt and pepper.
- With paper towel, clean edges of baking dish and cover with foil. Bake for 30 minutes, remove dish from oven and sprinkle onion rings over top. Return to oven and cook for 15 minutes. Serves 6.

Savory Beef Patties

1½ pounds lean ground beef
½ cup chili sauce
½ cup buttery cracker crumbs
1 (10 ounce) can beef broth
1 (6.8 ounce) packet beef-flavored rice

- Combine beef, chili sauce and cracker crumbs and form into 5 or 6 patties. In skillet, brown patties and pour beef broth over patties. Bring to a boil, reduce heat to low and simmer for 35 minutes.
- Prepare rice according to package directions and place on serving plate. Cover rice with patties and serve. Serves 6.

Southern Taco Pie

1 pound lean ground beef
1 large bell pepper, seeded, chopped
2 jalapeno peppers, seeded, chopped
1 (15 ounce) can Mexican stewed tomatoes
1 tablespoon chili powder
1 (8 ounce) package shredded sharp cheddar cheese
1 (8 ounce) box corn muffin mix
1 egg
⅓ cup milk

- Preheat oven to 375°.
- Brown ground beef, bell pepper and jalapeno peppers in large skillet with a little oil; drain. Stir in tomatoes, chili powder, ½ cup water and a little salt. Cover and cook on medium heat for about 10 minutes or until most liquid cooks out, but not dry.
- Pour into sprayed 9 x 13-inch baking pan and sprinkle with cheese.
- Combine corn muffin mix with egg and milk and pour over pie. Bake for 20 to 25 minutes or until muffin mix is light brown. Serves 6.

Look upon the beauty of the Lord. Psalm 27:4

Tex-Mex Supper

1 pound lean ground beef
1 large onion, chopped
1 (15 ounce) can pinto beans, drained
2 teaspoons cumin
½ head lettuce, torn
2 large tomatoes, chopped, drained
2 avocados, peeled, diced
1 (8 ounce) package shredded cheddar cheese
2 cups original corn chips
1 (8 ounce) bottle Catalina salad dressing

- Saute beef and onion in skillet. Drain grease and add beans, cumin, a little salt and pepper and ½ cup water and simmer until liquid cooks out.

- In large serving bowl, combine lettuce, tomatoes and avocados and toss.

- When ready to serve, toss salad with warm beef mixture, cheese, chips and dressing. Serves 8.

TIP: Have your beef-bean mixture cooked and remaining ingredients "ready" to take to church. Toss all together just before time to eat.

Make, Bake & Take: Beef

The firm foundation of God stands. Second Timothy 2:19

Taco Pie

1 pound lean ground beef
1 (11 ounce) can Mexicorn®, drained
1 (8 ounce) can tomato sauce
1 (1.25 ounce) packet taco seasoning
1 (9 inch) frozen piecrust
1½ cups shredded cheddar cheese, divided

- Preheat oven to 350°.

- In large skillet, brown and cook ground beef until no longer pink. Stir in corn, tomato sauce and taco seasoning. Keep warm.

- Place piecrust in pie pan, trim edges and bake 5 minutes. Remove from oven and spoon ground beef mixture onto piecrust, spreading evenly.

- Sprinkle 1 cup cheese over top and bake for 20 minutes or until filling is bubbly. Remove from oven, cover with remaining cheese and return to oven for 5 minutes. When serving, cut pie in wedges. Serves 6 to 8.

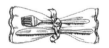

Good will come to him who is generous and lends freely. Psalm 112:5

Cheesy Meatball Pie

2 cups shredded hash brown potatoes, thawed
1 (10 ounce) box frozen green peas, thawed
18 frozen Italian meatballs, thawed, halved
¾ cup shredded cheddar cheese
½ cup biscuit mix
1 cup milk
2 large eggs

- Preheat oven to 375°.
- In bowl, toss hash brown potatoes with a little salt and pepper and spread in sprayed deep-dish pie plate. Layer peas, meatballs and cheese over potatoes in pie plate.
- In bowl, whisk biscuit mix, milk and eggs until ingredients blend well.
- Pour over layers of potato-cheese mixture and bake uncovered for 35 minutes or until center sets and top is golden brown. Let stand 10 minutes before cutting in wedges to serve. Serves 8 to 10.

Do to others as you would have them do to you. Luke 6:31

Tasty Taco Casserole

2 pounds lean ground beef
1 (10 ounce) can taco sauce
2 (15 ounce) cans Spanish rice
1 (8 ounce) can whole kernel corn, drained
1 (8 ounce) package shredded Mexican 4-cheese blend, divided
1 cup crushed tortilla chips

- Preheat oven to 350°.

- In skillet, brown beef, cook and stir until beef is crumbly. Add taco sauce, rice, corn and half cheese and mix well. Spoon into sprayed 9 x 13-inch baking pan, cover and bake for 35 minutes.

- Remove from oven, sprinkle remaining cheese and chips over top of casserole and continue baking for 5 minutes. Serves 8.

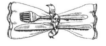

Do to others what you would have them do to you. Matthew 7:12

Spicy Onion-Mushroom Steak

1½ pounds tenderized round steak
Flour
1 (15 ounce) can Mexican stewed tomatoes
¾ cup picante sauce
1 (14 ounce) can beef broth
1 (6.4 ounce) package Mexican-style rice

- Cut round steak into serving-size pieces and dredge in
  flour. Brown steak in skillet with a little oil and stir in
  tomatoes, picante and beef broth. Bring to a boil, reduce heat to low, cover and simmer for 50 to 60 minutes.

- Prepare rice according to package directions and spoon
  onto serving platter. Spoon steak and sauce over rice.
  Serves 8.

Smothered Steak and Potatoes

1 (1½ pound) round steak
2 (15 ounce) cans whole new potatoes, drained
1 (10 ounce) can golden mushroom soup
1 (1 ounce) packet dry onion soup mix
1½ cups milk

- Preheat oven to 325°.

- Cut steak into serving-size pieces and brown in skillet
  with a little oil on high heat. Transfer to sprayed 9 x 13-
  inch baking pan and place potatoes over steak.

- In saucepan, combine mushroom soup, dry onion soup
  mix and milk and heat just enough to be able to mix
  well. Pour over steak and potatoes. Cover and bake for
  50 minutes. Serves 6.

Shepherd's Pie

1 pound boneless sirloin, cut into 1-inch cubes
1 onion, sliced
1 (8 ounce) can sliced carrots, drained
1 (14 ounce) jar tomato-pasta sauce
½ (7.2 ounce) box (1 pouch) roasted-garlic mashed potatoes
⅔ cup milk
2 tablespoons butter

- Preheat oven to 375°.
- Heat large non-stick skillet over medium heat and add beef cubes, onion and a little salt and pepper. Cook 10 minutes and stir frequently until beef browns.
- Stir in carrots, pasta sauce and ½ cup water and bring to a boil. Reduce heat to medium, cook 10 minutes and stir occasionally. Spread in sprayed 3-quart round baking dish.
- Prepare potatoes according to package directions. Use 1 pouch potatoes, 1 cup water, milk and butter. Spoon 8 mounds around edge of hot beef mixture.
- Bake for 25 minutes or until bubbly and potatoes are light golden brown. Serves 10.

You will know the truth, and the truth will set you free. John 8:32

Make, Bake & Take: Beef

Classy Beef and Noodles

2 pounds lean round steak, cut in strips
2 (10 ounce) cans golden mushroom soup
½ cup cooking sherry
1 (1 ounce) packet dry onion-mushroom soup mix
1 (12 ounce) package medium egg noodles
¼ cup (½ stick) butter

- Preheat oven to 325°.

- In skillet with a little oil, brown steak strips and drain off fat. Stir in mushroom soup, sherry, dry onion-mushroom soup mix and ¾ cup water. Spoon into sprayed 3-quart baking dish, cover and bake for 1 hour or until steak is tender.

- Cook noodles according to package directions, drain and stir in butter. Spoon onto serving platter and spoon steak mixture over noodles. Serves 8 to 10.

Dutch-Oven Roast

1 (3 pound) rump roast
1 onion, sliced
1 (10 ounce) can golden mushroom soup
1 (1 ounce) packet brown gravy mix
2 teaspoons minced garlic

- Preheat oven to 325°.

- Place roast in sprayed Dutch oven or large, heavy pot and place onion slices on top of roast.

- In saucepan, combine soup, gravy mix, garlic and ⅔ cup water and heat just enough for mixture to blend well. Pour mixture over roast.

- Place lid on Dutch oven or pot and bake for 3 hours 30 minutes or until roast is tender. Serves 8 to 10.

Reuben Casserole Supper

1 (20 ounce) bag frozen hash brown potatoes, thawed
1½ pounds (¼-inch) thick deli corned beef slices
1 (8 ounce) bottle Russian salad dressing, divided
1 (15 ounce) can sauerkraut, drained
8 slices Swiss cheese

- Preheat oven to 400°.
- Place hash brown potatoes in sprayed 9 x 13-inch baking dish and season with a little salt and pepper. Bake uncovered for 30 minutes.
- Place corned beef slices, overlapping on top of potatoes, spoon half bottle of dressing over top of beef and arrange sauerkraut on top.
- Cover with slices of cheese, reduce heat to 350° and bake another 15 minutes. Serves 8 to 10.

Broccoli-Rice and Ham Supper

1 (14 ounce) can chicken broth
1 (10 ounce) package frozen broccoli florets, thawed
1 carrot, shredded
1¼ cups instant rice
2 teaspoons lemon juice
1½ cups cooked ham, cut in strips
Lemon slices

- In large saucepan over high heat, bring broth to a boil. Add broccoli, carrots and rice and return to a boil. Reduce heat to low, cover and cook 5 minutes.
- Remove from heat, stir in rice, lemon juice and ham. Cover and let stand 5 minutes or until liquid absorbs. Fluff rice with fork and add a little salt and pepper.
- Transfer to serving bowl and garnish with twisted lemon slices. Serves 6.

Mac 'n Cheese Casserole

4 eggs
1½ cups milk
1 (12 ounce) package macaroni, cooked
1 (8 ounce) package shredded cheddar cheese
2 cups cubed ham
¾ cup seasoned breadcrumbs
¼ cup (½ stick) butter, cubed

- Preheat oven to 350°.
- In large bowl, lightly beat eggs and milk with a little salt and pepper. Stir in macaroni, cheese and ham.
- Spoon into sprayed 7 x 11-inch baking dish and bake uncovered for 20 minutes. Remove from oven, sprinkle with breadcrumbs and dot with butter. Continue baking another 15 minutes. Serves 8.

Ham Supper Quick

1 (4.6 ounce) box boil-in-bag broccoli and cheese rice
2 cups cooked, cubed ham
1 (10 ounce) can creamy chicken verde soup
1 (10 ounce) package frozen green peas, thawed
1 cup shredded cheddar cheese

- Preheat oven to 325°.
- Prepare rice according to package directions, but omit butter. In large bowl, combine cooked rice, ham, chicken verde soup and peas. Stir well.
- Spoon into sprayed 3-quart baking dish, cover and bake for 20 minutes. Remove from oven, sprinkle cheese over top of casserole and return to oven for 5 minutes. Serves 6 to 8.

 Ham for a Bunch

1 (12 - 20 pound) whole ham, fully cooked
Whole cloves
2 tablespoons dry mustard
1 (12 ounce) jar apricot preserves
1½ cups packed brown sugar

- Preheat oven to 450°.
- Place ham on rack in large roasting pan. Insert cloves in ham about 1-inch apart.
- In bowl, combine dry mustard and preserves and spread over entire surface of ham. Pat brown sugar over mustard-preserve mixture.
- Reduce heat to 325° and bake uncovered for 15 minutes per pound. Serves 8 to 15, depending on size of ham.

TIP: By placing ham in a very hot oven, the ham begins the cooking process sooner.

How great is the love the Father has lavished on us, that we should be called children of God! First John 3:1

Ham-Vegetable Supper

1½ cups dry corkscrew macaroni
1 (16 ounce) package frozen broccoli, cauliflower and carrots
1 (10 ounce) can broccoli-cheese soup
1 (3 ounce) package cream cheese with chives, softened
¾ cup milk
1 (8 ounce) package cubed Velveeta® cheese
1 tablespoon dijon-style mustard
2 cups cooked, cubed ham

- In large saucepan, cook macaroni according to package directions. For last 5 minutes of cooking time, bring back to boiling, add vegetables and cook remaining 5 minutes. Drain in colander.

- In same saucepan, combine soup, cream cheese, milk, cheese and mustard over low heat and stir until cream cheese melts.

- Gently stir in ham, macaroni-vegetable mixture and a little salt and pepper. Heat thoroughly and stir often. Transfer to 3-quart serving dish. Serves 8.

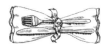

He who seeks good, finds goodwill. Proverbs 11:27

Ham and Corn Casserole

Ham and corn are always popular at church suppers
and this recipe is so easy to make.

2 cups baking mix
2 cups finely chopped, cooked ham
1 cup shredded cheddar cheese
¼ cup (½ stick) butter, melted
1 small onion, chopped
1 bell pepper, seeded, finely chopped
3 large eggs, slightly beaten
1 (15 ounce) can cream-style corn
1 (11 ounce) can Mexicorn®
3 fresh green onions, finely chopped

- Preheat oven to 350°.
- In large bowl, combine all ingredients except green onions. Pour into sprayed 7 x 11-inch baking dish and bake uncovered for 50 minutes or until golden brown and set.
- Cut into squares to serve. Garnish with chopped green onions. Serves 8 to 10.

He who watches over you will not slumber. Psalm 121:3

🗒 Ham and Pasta Bake

1 (10 ounce) can broccoli-cheese soup
½ cup grated parmesan cheese
1 cup milk
1 tablespoon spicy brown mustard
1 (16 ounce) package frozen broccoli florets, thawed
2 cups shell macaroni, cooked
8 ounces (deli) cooked ham, cut in bite-size chunks
Thin strips sweet red bell pepper for garnish

- In large skillet, combine soup, parmesan cheese, milk and mustard and mix well. Add broccoli and stir over medium heat.

- Reduce heat to low, cover and cook 5 minutes or until broccoli is tender-crisp.

- Stir in macaroni and ham and heat thoroughly. Transfer to sprayed 2-quart microwave dish so it can be reheated, if needed, when you get to church.

- Garnish with very thin strips of bell pepper. Serves 8 to 10.

There is a time to be silent and a time to speak. Ecclesiastes 3:7

Sweet-and-Sour Pork Chops

¾ cup flour
8 boneless (½ inch) thick boneless pork chops
4 tablespoons (½ stick) butter, divided
¾ cup orange juice
⅓ cup Craisins®
1 tablespoon dijon-style mustard
2 tablespoons brown sugar
2 (3.5 ounce) bags boil-in-bag rice

- Place flour in shallow bowl and dredge chops in flour. Brown pork chops, turning once, in heavy skillet with 2 tablespoons butter.

- Add orange juice, Craisins®, mustard, brown sugar and remaining butter. Cook on high heat until mixture bubbles and reduce heat. Cover and simmer 15 minutes.

- Cook rice according to package directions and place on serving platter. Place pork chops on top and serve with sauce. Serves 8.

Pork Chops and Potatoes

6 - 8 (bone-in) pork chops
2 (15 ounce) cans whole new potatoes, drained
2 (1 ounce) packets dry onion gravy mix
1 (14 ounce) can chicken broth

- Preheat oven to 325°.

- Brown pork chops in large skillet and place in sprayed 9 x 13-inch baking pan. Add potatoes to pork chops in baking pan.

- Place dry gravy mix in bowl, stir in about one-fourth of broth and mix well. Stir in remaining broth and pour over pork chops and potatoes. Cover and bake for 45 minutes. Serves 6 to 8.

Stuffed Pork Chops

4 (¾ inch) thick boneless center-cut pork chops

Stuffing:
2 slices rye bread, diced
⅓ cup chopped onion
⅓ cup chopped celery
⅓ cup dried apples, diced
⅓ cup chicken broth
½ teaspoon dried thyme

- Preheat oven to 400°.
- Make 1-inch wide slit on side of each chop and insert knife blade to other side, but not through pork chop. Sweep knife back and forth and carefully cut pocket opening larger.
- In bowl, combine rye bread pieces, onion, celery, apples, broth and thyme and mix well. Stuff chops with stuffing mixture and press to use all stuffing mixture in pork chops.
- Place chops in heavy skillet with a little oil and saute each chop about 3 minutes on each side. Transfer to non-stick baking dish and bake uncovered for 15 minutes. Serves 4.

For the Lord God is a sun and a shield. Psalm 84:11

Make, Bake & Take: Pork

Crunchy Pork Chops

1 cup crushed saltine crackers
¼ cup biscuit mix
¾ teaspoon seasoned salt
1 egg, beaten
5 - 6 (½ inch) thick boneless pork chops

- In shallow bowl, combine crushed crackers, biscuit mix and seasoned salt. In second shallow bowl, combine beaten egg and 2 tablespoons water.
- Dip pork chops into egg mixture and dredge in cracker mixture.
- Heat a little oil in heavy skillet, cook pork chops about 15 minutes and turn once. Serves 5 to 6.

Choice Tenderloin Slices

2 (1 pound) pork tenderloins
1 (12 ounce) jar apricot preserves
⅓ cup lemon juice
⅓ cup ketchup
1 tablespoon light soy sauce
2 cups cooked instant rice

- Preheat oven to 325°.
- Place tenderloins in sprayed 7 x 11-inch baking pan. In saucepan, combine preserves, lemon juice, ketchup and soy sauce and heat just until mixture blends well.
- Spoon sauce over tenderloins, cover and bake for 1 hour. Baste twice during cooking.
- Let tenderloins rest about 15 minutes before slicing. Place slices and sauce over hot, cooked rice. Serves 6 to 8.

Spicy Glazed Pork Tenderloin

½ cup orange juice
¼ cup lime juice
½ cup packed brown sugar
1 teaspoon ground cumin
2 (1 pound) pork tenderloins

- In small bowl, combine orange juice, lime juice, brown sugar and cumin.
- Pat tenderloins dry with paper towels and season with a little salt and pepper. Place a little oil in large skillet over medium-high heat.
- Cook tenderloins, turn and brown on all sides, about 9 to 10 minutes total. Reduce heat to medium, add orange juice mixture and cook until mixture is thick and syrupy, about 10 minutes.
- Transfer to cutting board, cover tenderloins with foil and let rest 10 minutes before slicing crosswise into ½-inch slices. Arrange on serving plate and pour glaze over slices. Serves 8.

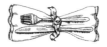

A man's steps are directed by the Lord. Proverbs 20:24

Garlic-Roasted Pork Tenderloin

2 (1 pound) pork tenderloins

Rub:
4 teaspoons minced garlic
1 tablespoon dijon-style mustard
1 tablespoon ketchup
1 tablespoon soy sauce
1 tablespoon honey

- Preheat oven to 350°.
- Place tenderloins on foil-lined roasting pan. Combine garlic, mustard, ketchup, soy sauce and honey and rub evenly over pork. Roast for 30 minutes or until thermometer inserted into thickest portion registers 155°.
- Remove from oven, cover with foil and let stand for 10 minutes.

Sauce:
2 teaspoons rice vinegar
2 teaspoons sesame oil
1 tablespoon soy sauce
¼ cup honey

- Combine all sauce ingredients. Slice pork diagonally and place on serving platter. Drizzle sauce over pork slices. Serves 8.

I wait for the Lord, my soul does wait and in His word do I hope. Psalm 130:5

Nutty Pork Loin

1 (3 - 4 pound) boneless pork loin roast
1 teaspoon Creole seasoning
⅔ cup orange juice
⅔ cup orange marmalade
⅓ cup smooth peanut butter

- Preheat oven to 350°.
- Place pork loin in roasting pan and season well with Creole seasoning. Cover and bake for 1 hour or until thermometer registers 160°.
- In saucepan, combine orange juice, marmalade and peanut butter. Heat just enough to mix well.
- Reduce oven heat to 325° and pour orange sauce over roast, cover and cook another 1 hour 30 minutes.
- Brush occasionally with sauce during last hour of cooking time. To serve, slice roast, place in serving dish and cover with orange sauce. Serves 8 to 10.

You cannot understand the work of God, the Maker of all things.
Ecclesiastes 11:5

Pork Chops Deluxe

1 cup rice
¼ cup flour
1 teaspoon seasoned salt
6 pork chops with bone
3 tablespoons oil, divided
1 onion, chopped
1 green bell pepper, seeded, chopped
1 (15 ounce) can Mexican stewed tomatoes
1 (10 ounce) can chicken broth

- Preheat oven to 325º.
- Place rice in sprayed 9 x 13-inch baking dish. Combine flour and seasoned salt in shallow bowl and dredge pork chops in flour mixture.
- Brown pork chops in large skillet with half oil and place on top of rice.
- With remaining oil, saute onion and bell pepper about 4 minutes. Add stewed tomatoes and chicken broth and mix well.
- Pour over pork chops in baking dish. Cover and bake for 1 hour. Serves 6.

The heavens declare the glory of God; the skies proclaim the work of his hands.
Psalm 19:1

Sausage-Bean Casserole

1 pound pork sausage
2 (15 ounce) cans pork and beans with liquid
1 (15 ounce) can Mexican stewed tomatoes
1 (8 ounce) package corn muffin mix
1 egg
⅓ cup milk

- Preheat oven to 350°.
- Brown sausage in large skillet and drain. Add beans and stewed tomatoes, stir and bring to a boil. Pour into sprayed 3-quart baking dish.
- Prepare muffin mix with egg and milk according to package directions. Drop by teaspoonfuls over meat-bean mixture and bake for 30 minutes or until top is light brown. Serves 8.

Sausage-Potato Bake

1 (10 ounce) can cream of celery soup
½ cup sour cream
1 teaspoon freeze-dried chives
1 cup shredded cheddar cheese
2 (15 ounce) cans whole new potatoes, halved, drained
1 (10 ounce) package frozen cut green beans, thawed
1 pound cooked Polish sausage, sliced
1 (2.8 ounce) can french-fried onions

- Preheat oven to 350°.
- Spray 7 x 11-inch baking dish. In large bowl, combine soup, sour cream, chives and cheese. Stir in potatoes, green beans and sausage and spoon into baking dish. Cover and bake for 30 minutes.
- Remove from oven and sprinkle onions over casserole. Bake for another 15 minutes or until onions are golden brown. Serves 8 to 10.

Colorful Sausage Supper

4 tablespoons olive oil, divided
1 pound Polish sausage, cut into ¼-inch slices
1 sweet red bell pepper, seeded, julienned
3 small zucchini, sliced
3 small yellow squash, sliced
1 (12 ounce) package penne pasta
1 (26 ounce) jar spaghetti sauce, heated

- In large skillet with 2 tablespoons oil, saute sausage, bell pepper, zucchini and squash until vegetables are tender-crisp. Keep warm.

- Cook pasta according to package directions and drain. Stir in remaining oil and add a little salt and pepper.

- Spoon into 9 x 13-inch baking dish and spread heated spaghetti sauce over pasta. Use slotted spoon to top with sausage-vegetable mixture. Serves 10 to 12.

TIP: Take dish containing pasta and sauce to the church. Cover and heat at 350° for about 10 minutes; then heat the sauce mixture and pour over pasta.

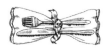

Command them to do good, to be rich in good deeds, and to be generous and willing to share. 1 Timothy 6:18

Sweet-and-Sour
Pork Loin Roast

4 - 5 pound pork loin roast
1 (12 ounce) bottle chili sauce
1 (12 ounce) jar apricot preserves
1 (20 ounce) can chunk pineapple, drained
2 bell peppers, seeded, sliced

- Preheat oven to 325º.
- Season roast with a little salt and pepper and brown in a little oil in large heavy roasting pan. Add ½ cup water to pan, cover and bake for 1 hour.
- Mix chili sauce and apricot preserves and pour over roast. Reduce heat to 275º and cook additional 2 hours.
- Add pineapple and bell pepper and cook for 15 minutes. Serves 10 to 12.

A man's steps are directed by the Lord. Proverbs 20:24

Shrimp and Chicken Curry

2 (10 ounce) cans cream of chicken soup
⅓ cup milk
1½ teaspoons curry powder
1 (12 ounce) can chicken breast, drained
2 (6 ounce) cans shrimp, drained
1 cup cooked rice

- In saucepan, heat soup, milk and curry powder. Stir in chicken pieces and shrimp. Heat, stirring constantly, until mixture is thoroughly hot.
- Serve over hot, cooked rice. Serves 6.

Tuna-Stuffed Tomatoes

4 large tomatoes
1 (12 ounce) cans white meat tuna, drained
2 cups chopped celery
½ cup chopped cashews
1 small zucchini with peel, chopped
½ - ⅔ cup mayonnaise

- Cut thin slice off top of each tomato, scoop out pulp and discard. Turn tomatoes over on paper towels to drain.
- Combine tuna, celery, cashews, zucchini and a little salt and pepper and mix well.
- Add ½ cup mayonnaise and blend. Add more mayonnaise if needed. Spoon mixture into hollowed-out tomatoes and chill. Serves 4.

May the God of hope fill you with all joy and peace as you trust in him.
Romans 15:13

Tuna-Pasta Casserole

1 (8 ounce) package elbow macaroni
1 (8 ounce) package shredded Velveeta® cheese
1 (12 ounce) can tuna, drained
1 (10 ounce) can cream of celery soup
1 cup milk

- Preheat oven to 350°.
- Cook macaroni according to package directions. Drain and stir in cheese until cheese melts.
- Stir in tuna, celery soup and milk and spoon into sprayed 7 x 11-inch baking dish. Cover and bake for 35 minutes or until bubbly. Serves 6.

Seasoned Breadsticks

1 (11 ounce) tube refrigerated breadsticks
¼ cup (½ stick) butter, melted
2 tablespoons prepared pesto
¼ teaspoon garlic powder
3 tablespoons grated parmesan cheese

- Preheat oven to 375°.
- Unroll, separate breadsticks and place on unsprayed baking pan. Combine melted butter, pesto and garlic powder and brush over breadsticks. Twist each bread-stick 3 times. Sprinkle with parmesan cheese.
- Bake for about 12 minutes or until golden brown. Serves 6 to 8.

Glorify the Lord with me; let us exalt his name together. Psalm 34:3

Monterey Breadsticks

1 (8 ounce) package shredded Monterey Jack cheese
¼ cup poppy seeds
2 tablespoons dry onion soup mix
⅛ teaspoon cayenne pepper
2 (11 ounce) cans breadstick dough

- Preheat oven to 375°.
- Spread cheese evenly in sprayed 9 x 13-inch baking pan. Sprinkle poppy seeds, soup mix and cayenne pepper. Stir mixture to evenly distribute cayenne pepper.
- Separate breadstick dough into sticks and stretch strips slightly until each strip is about 12 inches long. Place strips, one at a time, into cheese mixture and turn to coat all sides.
- Cut into 3 or 4-inch strips, place on second baking pan and bake for 12 to 14 minutes or until sticks are light brown. Serves 6 to 12.

Deluxe Parmesan Bread

1 (16 ounce) loaf unsliced Italian bread
½ cup refrigerated creamy Caesar salad dressing
2 tablespoons mayonnaise
⅓ cup grated parmesan cheese
3 tablespoons finely chopped green onions

- Cut 24 (½-inch) thick slices from bread. In small bowl, combine dressing, mayonnaise, parmesan cheese and onions and spread 1 heaping teaspoon dressing mixture onto each slice of bread.
- Place bread on baking sheet and broil 4 inches from heat until golden brown. Watch closely so that toast does not burn. Serve immediately. Serves 6 to 12.

Sticky Sweet Rolls

1 (12 count) package frozen dinner rolls, partially thawed
¼ cup (½ stick) butter, melted
¾ cup packed brown sugar
½ teaspoon ground cinnamon
1 cup chopped pecans

- Place 1 roll in each of 12 sprayed muffin cups and cut a deep "x" in top of each roll. Spray tops of rolls with cooking spray and place sheet of plastic wrap over rolls.

- Let rise about 3 hours or until double in size.

- Preheat oven to 350°.

- In bowl, combine butter, brown sugar and cinnamon and mix well.

- Stir in pecans and spoon sugar mixture over rolls. Pull "x" open and let sugar mixture seep into rolls.

- Bake for 15 to 20 minutes or until light brown. Serve 6 to 8.

Blessed is the man who perseveres under trial ... he will receive a crown of life.
James 1:12

Texas Cornbread

1 cup yellow cornmeal
⅔ cup flour
¼ teaspoon baking soda
1¼ cups buttermilk*
1 large egg, beaten

- Preheat oven to 400°.
- Combine cornmeal, flour and baking soda in center of bowl and stir in buttermilk and egg just until moist.
- Pour into sprayed 7 x 11-inch baking pan and bake for 15 minutes or until golden brown. Serves 6 to 8.

TIP: To make buttermilk, mix 1 cup milk with 1 tablespoon lemon juice or vinegar and let milk rest about 10 minutes.

Green Chile-Cheese Bread

1 (16 ounce) loaf unsliced Italian bread
½ cup (1 stick) butter, melted
1 tablespoon mayonnaise
1 (7 ounce) can chopped green chilies, drained
1 cup shredded Monterey Jack cheese

- Preheat oven to 350°.
- Slice bread ½-inch thick almost all the way through.
- Combine butter, mayonnaise, green chilies and cheese and spread between bread slices. Wrap loaf securely with heavy foil and bake for 20 minutes. Serves 6 to 12.

Clothe yourselves with my compassion, kindness, humility, gentleness and patience. Colossians 3:12

Crunchy Corn Sticks

2 cups biscuit mix
2 tablespoons cornmeal
⅛ teaspoon cayenne pepper
3 tablespoons finely minced green onions
1 (8 ounce) can cream-style corn
½ cup (1 stick) butter, melted

- Preheat oven to 400°.
- Combine biscuit mix, cornmeal, cayenne pepper, onions and cream-style corn and mix until they blend well. Place dough on floured surface and pat out to ½-inch thickness. Cut into strips and roll in melted butter.
- Place on cookie sheet and bake for 15 to 16 minutes or until light brown. Serves 6 to 10.

Corny Sausage Squares

½ pound pork sausage
1 (10 ounce) can condensed golden corn soup
2 eggs
¼ cup milk
1 (8 ounce) package corn muffin mix

- Preheat oven to 350°.
- Brown sausage and stir until sausage is crumbly. Drain and set aside. In medium bowl combine soup, eggs and milk. Stir in corn muffin mix until it blends. Fold in sausage and pour into sprayed 9-inch square baking pan.
- Bake for 25 minutes or until golden brown and cut into squares to serve. Serves 8.

Hide me in the shadows of your wings. Psalm 17:8

Cheesy Breadsticks

1 loaf thick sliced bread
¾ cup (1½ sticks) butter, melted
1 cup shredded cheddar cheese
1 teaspoon Italian seasoning
1 teaspoon paprika

- Preheat oven to 325°.
- Remove crust from bread (discard crusts) and slice into 1-inch sticks. Brush or roll each stick in melted butter and place, close together, on large baking sheet. Sprinkle cheese, Italian seasoning and paprika over sticks and separate sticks so that all sides of stick will toast.
- Bake for 20 minutes or until sticks are slightly brown and lightly toasted. Serves 6 to 12.

Cheese-Toasted French Bread

1 (16 ounce) loaf unsliced French bread
1 (3 ounce) package bacon bits
1 (8 ounce) package shredded mozzarella cheese
½ cup (1 stick) butter, melted

- Preheat oven to 350°.
- Slice loaf of bread into 1-inch slices and place sliced loaf on large piece of foil.
- Combine bacon and cheese and sprinkle mixture in between slices of bread.
- Drizzle melted butter over loaf and let some drip down in between slices. Wrap loaf tightly in foil. Bake for 20 to 25 minutes or until thoroughly hot. Serves 8 to 12.

Be joyful in hope, patient in affliction, faithful in prayer. Romans 12:12

Buttered Ranch-Style Bread

1 (16 ounce) loaf unsliced French bread
½ cup (1 stick) butter, softened
1 tablespoon dry ranch-style dressing mix
2 tablespoons mayonnaise
3 tablespoons bacon bits

- Preheat oven to 350°.
- Cut loaf in half horizontally.
- Combine butter, dressing mix, mayonnaise and bacon bits and mix well. Spread mixture on bottom and top sides of bread.
- Place top back on bottom of loaf, wrap securely with heavy foil and bake for 20 to 25 minutes. Serves 8 to 12.

Swiss Bread Slices

1 (1 pound) loaf unsliced French bread
1 (8 ounce) package shredded Swiss cheese
⅓ cup mayonnaise
2 teaspoons minced fresh basil
1 tablespoon finely grated onion
1 tablespoon olive oil
1 teaspoon cider vinegar

- Preheat oven to 375°.
- Cut bread in half lengthwise. In bowl, combine cheese, mayonnaise, basil, onion, olive oil and vinegar.
- Spread over cut sides of bread and place on unsprayed baking sheet.
- Bake for 8 to 10 minutes or until cheese melts and bread is light brown. When ready to serve, cut loaf into 6-8 equal portions. Serves 6 to 8.

Herb Pull-Apart Bread

½ cup (1 stick) butter
1 teaspoon dried basil leaves
1½ teaspoons parsley flakes
½ teaspoon dried thyme leaves
½ teaspoon cilantro leaves
1 teaspoon garlic powder
1 (3 pound) package frozen, white dinner roll dough

- In saucepan, combine butter, basil, parsley, thyme, cilantro and garlic powder and heat on low heat until herbs blend with melted butter.

- Spray 12-cup bundt pan, place 12 frozen dough balls in pan and generously brush with half butter mixture.

- Layer 12 more dough balls in pan and brush with remaining butter mixture. Cover and let stand in warm place about 4 hours or until double in size.

- Preheat oven to 350°. Bake for 24 to 27 minutes or until bread sounds hollow when tapped and top is golden brown.

- Cool 5 minutes and turn upside down onto serving plate. Serves 10 to 14.

Make, Bake & Take: Breads

A cheerful look brings joy to the heart. Proverbs 15:30

Holiday Bread

3 cups flour
1 (8 ounce) package shredded Italian-style cheese blend
2 teaspoons baking powder
½ teaspoon garlic powder
3 eggs, beaten
1 (5 ounce) can evaporated milk
3 fresh green onions, finely chopped
¼ cup (½ stick) butter, melted
¼ cup oil-packed, sun-dried tomatoes, drained, minced
1 egg yolk

- Preheat oven to 350°.
- In large bowl, combine flour, cheese, baking powder, a little salt and garlic powder.
- Add eggs, evaporated milk, green onions, melted butter and sun-dried tomatoes. Mix until they blend well.
- Place dough onto lightly floured surface. Knead dough by folding and gently pressing dough for about 12 strokes or until it holds together.
- Divide dough into 3 equal pieces. Roll each piece into 1 (14 inch) rope. On sprayed baking sheet, line ropes 1-inch apart. Braid ropes, pinching ends to seal.
- Combine egg yolk and 1 tablespoon water and brush on top of bread.
- Bake about 40 minutes or until golden brown. Place on wire rack to cool. Serves 10 to 12.

Do everything without complaining or arguing. Philippians 2:14

Sour Cream Biscuits

2 cups plus 1 tablespoon flour
3 teaspoons baking powder
½ teaspoon baking soda
½ cup shortening
1 (8 ounce) carton sour cream

- Preheat oven to 400°.
- Combine dry ingredients, add a little salt and cut in shortening.
- Gradually add sour cream and mix lightly. Turn on lightly floured board and knead a few times.
- Roll to ½-inch thickness. Cut with biscuit cutter and place on sprayed baking sheet.
- Bake for 15 minutes or until light brown. Serves 4 to 6.

Supper Biscuits

5 cups biscuit mix
1 cup finely shredded cheddar cheese
1 (14 ounce) can chicken broth with roasted garlic

- Preheat oven to 400°.
- Stir biscuit mix, cheese and broth until it forms a soft dough. Drop by heaping spoonfuls onto sprayed baking sheet.
- Bake for 10 to 12 minutes or until biscuits are light brown. Serve 6 to 12.

Pleasant words are honeycomb, sweet to the soul and healing to the bones.
Proverbs 16:24

Creamy Rich Biscuits

2 cups flour
3 teaspoons baking powder
1 (8 ounce) carton whipping cream

- Preheat oven to 375°.
- Combine flour, baking powder and ¾ teaspoon salt in mixing bowl. Beat whipping cream just until it holds its shape and stir, using a fork, into flour mixture.
- Place dough on lightly floured board and knead for 1 minute. Pat dough to ¾-inch thickness and cut biscuits with medium biscuit cutter.
- Place on sprayed baking sheet and bake for 14 to 16 minutes or until light brown. Serves 4 to 8.

Quick Onion Biscuits

2 cups biscuit mix
¼ cup milk
1 (8 ounce) container French onion dip
2 tablespoons finely minced green onion

- Preheat oven to 400°.
- In mixing bowl, combine biscuit mix, milk, onion dip and green onions and mix until soft dough forms. Drop dough by heaping teaspoonfuls onto sprayed baking sheet.
- Bake for 10 to 12 minutes or until golden brown. Serves 6 to 8.

For if you forgive men when they sin against you, your heavenly Father will also forgive you. Matthew 6:14

Asparagus Casserole

3 (15 ounce) cans cut asparagus, drained
3 eggs, hard-boiled, sliced
½ cup chopped pecans
1 (10 ounce) can cream of asparagus soup
½ cup milk
1 cup shredded Swiss cheese

- Preheat oven to 350°.

- Place asparagus in sprayed 7 x 11-inch baking dish and top with sliced eggs and pecans.

- In saucepan, combine soup, milk and Swiss cheese and heat over medium heat, stirring constantly, just until mixture blends well.

- Pour over asparagus mixture and spread to cover casserole. Cover and bake for 25 minutes or until casserole is bubbly around edges. Serves 8.

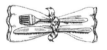

Stop judging by mere appearances and make a right judgment.
John 7:24

Cheddar-Broccoli Bake

1 (10 ounce) can cheddar cheese soup
1 (8 ounce) package shredded cheddar Jack cheese
⅓ cup milk
1 teaspoon seasoned salt
2 ribs celery, chopped
1 sweet red bell pepper, julienned
1 (16 ounce) bag frozen broccoli florets, cooked, drained
1 (2.8 ounce) can french-fried onion rings

- Preheat oven to 325°.
- In bowl, combine soup, cheese, milk, salt, celery, bell pepper and broccoli and mix well. Pour into sprayed 3-quart baking dish.
- Cover and bake for 25 minutes. Uncover, sprinkle onion rings over casserole and return to oven for 10 to 15 minutes or until onion rings are golden. Serves 8.

Jazzy Cheesy Broccoli

1 (24 ounce) package frozen broccoli florets, thawed
1 (10 ounce) can cream of celery soup
¾ cup milk
½ teaspoon garlic powder
⅛ teaspoon cayenne pepper
1½ cups cubed Velveeta® cheese

- Place broccoli in microwave-safe bowl and microwave on HIGH about 4 minutes or until tender. Keep warm.
- In saucepan, combine celery soup, milk, garlic powder and cayenne pepper. Heat and stir to mix well. On low heat, stir in cheese until it melts. Remove from heat.
- Place broccoli in serving bowl and spoon cheese sauce over broccoli. Serves 8 to 10.

Broccoli Frittata

3 tablespoons butter
½ cup chopped onion
4 cups fresh broccoli florets without stems
6 large eggs, slightly beaten
1 (1 ounce) packet cream of broccoli soup mix
¾ cup shredded cheddar cheese
½ cup milk

- Preheat oven to 350°.
- In skillet, melt butter and saute onion. Add broccoli and 1 tablespoon water.
- Cook, stirring occasionally, on low heat for about 5 minutes until tender-crisp, but still bright green.
- In separate bowl, whisk eggs, soup mix, cheese, milk and a little salt and pepper. Fold in broccoli-onion mixture.
- Pour into sprayed 10-inch deep-dish pie pan and bake for 20 to 25 minutes or until center is set.
- Let frittata stand for 5 to 10 minutes before cutting into wedges. Serves 8.

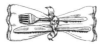

Serve the Lord with gladness: come before his presence with singing.
Psalm 100:2

Impossible Broccoli Pie

1 (16 ounce) package frozen broccoli florets, thawed
1 (12 ounce) package shredded cheddar cheese, divided
½ cup chopped onion
3 eggs, slightly beaten
¾ cup buttermilk biscuit mix
1½ cups milk

- Preheat oven to 350°.
- Cut large chunks of broccoli into smaller pieces and discard some stems.
- In large mixing bowl, combine broccoli, two-thirds of cheese and onion and mix well. Spoon into sprayed 10-inch, deep-dish pie pan.
- In same mixing bowl, mix eggs and biscuit mix and beat for several minutes. Add milk and mix until fairly smooth. Pour over broccoli and cheese mixture.
- Bake uncovered for 35 to 40 minutes or until knife inserted in center comes out clean.
- Top with remaining cheese and bake just until cheese melts. Let stand 5 minutes before slicing into wedges to serve. Serves 10.

O Lord, our Lord, how majestic is your name in all the earth.
Psalm 8:1

Broccoli-Cauliflower Casserole

1 (10 ounce) box frozen broccoli florets, thawed
1 (10 ounce) box frozen cauliflower, thawed
1 egg, beaten
⅔ cup mayonnaise
1 (10 ounce) can cream of chicken soup
¼ cup milk
1 cup shredded Swiss cheese
1½ cups seasoned breadcrumbs
2 tablespoons butter, melted

- Preheat oven to 350°.
- Cook broccoli and cauliflower in microwave according to package directions. Drain well and place in large mixing bowl.
- In saucepan, combine egg, mayonnaise, soup, milk and cheese and mix well. Heat just enough to be able to mix.
- Spoon into mixing bowl with broccoli-cauliflower and gently mix. Pour into sprayed 2½-quart baking dish.
- Combine breadcrumbs and butter, sprinkle over broccoli and cauliflower mixture and bake for 35 minutes. Serves 6 to 8.

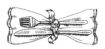

Blessed are the poor in spirit, for theirs is the kingdom of heaven.
Matthew 5:3

Make, Bake & Take: Vegetables

Baked Cauliflower

2 (16 ounce) packages frozen cauliflower, thawed
2 eggs, slightly beaten
1⅓ cups mayonnaise
2 (10 ounce) cans cream of chicken soup
1 (8 ounce) package shredded Swiss cheese
2 ribs celery, sliced
2 green bell peppers, chopped
2½ cups round buttery cracker crumbs
Paprika

- Preheat oven to 350°.
- Spray 11 x 14-inch baking dish, place cauliflower in dish and cover with plastic wrap, but leave 1 corner open.
- Microwave on HIGH for 3 minutes. Turn dish and cook another 2 minutes.
- In medium saucepan, combine eggs, mayonnaise, chicken soup and cheese. Heat just until it mixes well. Add celery and bell pepper to cauliflower and mix well.
- Pour soup mixture over vegetables and spread evenly. Cover with cracker crumbs and bake for 35 to 40 minutes or until cracker crumbs are light brown.
- Sprinkle paprika over top of casserole before serving. Serves 10 to 12.

Everyone should be quick to listen, slow to speak and slow to become angry. James 1:19

Make, Bake & Take: Vegetables

Sunny Day Carrots

2½ cups finely shredded carrots
2 cups cooked white rice
2 eggs, beaten
1 (8 ounce) package shredded Velveeta® cheese
1 (15 ounce) can cream-style corn
¼ cup whipping cream
2 tablespoons butter, melted
2 tablespoons dried minced onion
1 teaspoon seasoned salt
½ teaspoon white pepper

- Preheat oven to 350°.
- Combine all ingredients in large bowl. Spoon into sprayed 3-quart baking dish.
- Bake uncovered for 40 minutes or until set. Serves 8.

Maple-Raisin Carrots

¼ cup (½ stick) butter
½ cup packed brown sugar
2 tablespoons maple syrup
1 (16 ounce) package baby carrots
⅓ cup golden raisins

- In large saucepan, combine butter, brown sugar, maple syrup and a little salt. Cook, uncovered, over medium heat for 3 to 4 minutes or until it thickens slightly.
- Stir in carrots and raisins and cook 10 more minutes or until carrots are tender. Serves 6 to 8.

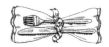

Fiesta Corn

1 (15 ounce) can cream-style corn
1 (15 ounce) can whole kernel corn
1 green bell pepper, seeded, chopped
1 (4 ounce) can chopped green chilies
¼ cup (½ stick) butter, melted
2 eggs, beaten
¼ teaspoon cayenne pepper
¼ teaspoon sugar
1½ cups buttery cracker crumbs, divided
1 cup shredded 4-cheese blend

- Preheat oven to 350°.

- In large bowl, combine both cans of corn, bell pepper, green chilies, butter, eggs, cayenne pepper, sugar, ½ cup cracker crumbs, cheese and a little salt and pepper.

- Spoon into sprayed 3-quart baking dish and sprinkle remaining crumbs on top. Bake uncovered for 35 minutes. Serves 6 to 8.

"For I know the plans that I have for you", declares the Lord, "plans to prosper you and not to harm you, plans to give you hope and a future." Jeremiah 29:11

Make, Bake & Take: Vegetables

Everybody's Favorite Corn

1 (15 ounce) can whole kernel corn
1 (15 ounce) can cream-style corn
½ cup (1 stick) butter, melted
2 eggs, beaten
1 (8 ounce) carton sour cream
1 (6 ounce) package jalapeno cornbread mix
½ cup shredded cheddar cheese

- Preheat oven to 350°.
- Mix all ingredients, except cheese, in large bowl and pour into sprayed 9 x 13-inch baking dish.
- Bake for 35 minutes or until light brown on top.
- Uncover, sprinkle cheese on top and return to oven for 5 minutes. Serves 8 to 10.

Creamed Onions and Peas

1 (10 ounce) can cream of celery soup
½ cup milk
3 (15 ounce) jars tiny white onions, drained
1 (10 ounce) package frozen peas
½ cup slivered almonds
3 tablespoons grated parmesan cheese

- Preheat oven to 350°.
- In large saucepan, combine soup and milk; heat and stir until bubbly. Gently stir in onions, peas and almonds and mix well.
- Spoon into sprayed 2-quart baking dish. Cover and bake for 30 minutes. Sprinkle parmesan cheese over top of casserole before serving. Serves 8.

TIP: For a little colorful garnish, sprinkle a little paprika over top of casserole.

Make, Bake & Take: Vegetables

 # Creamed Vegetable Bake

1 (16 ounce) package frozen broccoli, cauliflower and carrots
1 (10 ounce) package frozen green peas
1 (10 ounce) package frozen whole kernel corn
2 (10 ounce) can cream of mushroom soup
1 (8 ounce) package cream cheese, cubed
⅔ cup milk
2 cups seasoned croutons

- Cook all vegetables according to package directions, drain and place in large mixing bowl.

- In saucepan, combine soup, cream cheese, milk and a little salt and pepper.

- Heat on medium-low heat and stir constantly until mixture blends well. Stir into vegetables in bowl and gently mix.

- Spoon into sprayed 3-quart baking dish and cover with croutons. Bake for 25 to 30 minutes or until croutons are light brown. Serves 10 to 12.

Therefore, as we have opportunity let us do good to all people.
Galatians 6:10

Creamy-Cheesy Zucchini

3 pounds zucchini, sliced
1 sweet red bell pepper, finely diced
¼ cup (½ stick) plus 3 tablespoons butter, melted
1 (10 ounce) can cream of celery soup
1 (8 ounce) package cubed Velveeta® cheese
1 teaspoon seasoned salt
2½ cups crushed buttery cheese crackers
⅓ cup slivered almonds

- Preheat oven to 325°.
- In saucepan, boil zucchini and bell pepper just until barely tender and drain well.
- Do not over cook! Combine ¼ cup (½ stick) melted butter, soup, cheese, ¼ cup water and salt.
- Gently stir in zucchini mixture and spoon into 3-quart baking dish. Sprinkle crushed crackers and almonds over top and drizzle 3 tablespoons melted butter over crackers.
- Bake uncovered for 35 minutes or until hot and bubbly. Serves 8 to 10.

Make, Bake & Take: Vegetables

I know that everything God does will endure forever; nothing can be added to it and nothing taken from it. Ecclesiastes 3:14

Sunday Green Beans

3 (15 ounce) cans whole green beans, drained
1 (16 ounce) package shredded Mexican Velveeta® cheese
1 (8 ounce) can sliced water chestnuts, drained, chopped
½ cup slivered almonds
¾ cup chopped, roasted red bell peppers
1½ cups cracker crumbs
¼ cup (½ stick) butter, melted

- Preheat oven to 350°.

- Place green beans in sprayed 9 x 13-inch baking dish and cover with shredded cheese. Sprinkle with water chestnuts, almonds and roasted bell peppers. Place casserole in microwave and heat just until cheese begins to melt.

- Combine cracker crumbs and melted butter, sprinkle over casserole and bake uncovered for 30 minutes. Serves 10 to 12.

Green Caesar Bake

2 pounds fresh green beans, snapped
1 (6 ounce) package garlic-flavored croutons, lightly crushed, divided
1½ cups bottled creamy Caesar-style salad dressing
⅓ cup grated parmesan cheese
1 tablespoon lemon juice

- Preheat oven to 350°.

- Place beans in saucepan with ½ cup water and bring to a boil. Cook about 8 minutes or until tender. Drain and rinse with cold water.

- Transfer beans to large bowl and stir in 1 cup croutons, salad dressing, cheese and lemon juice. Spoon into sprayed 7 x 11-inch baking dish. Top with remaining croutons and bake for 30 minutes or until croutons are golden brown. Serves 10.

Fancy Green Beans

2 (16 ounce) package frozen French-style green beans,
   thawed
½ cup (1 stick) butter
1 (8 ounce) package fresh mushrooms, sliced
2 (10 ounce) cans cream of chicken soup
⅔ cup sliced roasted red bell peppers
2 teaspoons soy sauce
1 cup shredded white cheddar cheese
⅔ cup chopped cashew nuts
⅔ cup chow mein noodles

- Preheat oven to 325°.
- Cook green beans according to package directions, drain and set aside. In large saucepan, melt butter and saute mushrooms about 5 minutes, but do not brown.
- Stir in soups, ¼ cup water, roasted peppers, soy sauce and cheese and gently mix.
- Fold in drained green beans and spoon into sprayed, deep 9 x 13-inch baking pan.
- Combine cashews and chow mein noodles, sprinkle over top of casserole and bake uncovered for 30 minutes or until edges are hot and bubbly. Serves 10 to 12.

Let us not love with words or tongue but with actions and in truth.
First John 3:18

Filled Summer Squash

5 large yellow squash
1 (16 ounce) package frozen chopped spinach
1 (8 ounce) package cream cheese, cubed
1 (1 ounce) packet dry onion soup mix
¾ cup shredded cheddar cheese

- Steam squash whole until tender. Slit squash length-wise and remove seeds with spoon.
- Cook spinach according to package directions and drain. When spinach is done, remove pan from heat, add cream cheese and stir until cream cheese melts. Stir in soup mix and blend well.
- Preheat oven to 325°. Place squash shells on large, sprayed baking pan. Fill shells with spinach mixture and top with heaping tablespoon of cheddar cheese. Bake for 10 to 15 minutes or until squash is thoroughly hot. Serves 5.

Italian White Beans

1 onion, coarsely chopped
1 bell pepper, seeded, chopped
2 teaspoons minced garlic
2 tablespoons olive oil
2 (15 ounce) cans great northern beans, drained
1 teaspoon sugar
1 teaspoon white wine vinegar
1 (16 ounce) roll prepared polenta
½ cup grated parmesan cheese

- In large saucepan, saute onion, bell pepper and garlic in olive oil. Stir in beans, sugar, vinegar and a little salt and pepper. Stir over medium heat several times until mixture is thoroughly hot.
- Serve over sliced, heated polenta and sprinkle with a little parmesan cheese. Serves 8.

Garden Casserole

1 pound yellow squash, sliced
1 pound zucchini, sliced
1 green and 1 red bell pepper, seeded, chopped
1 (15 ounce) can sliced carrots, drained
1 (10 ounce) can cream of chicken soup
1 (8 ounce) carton sour cream
½ cup (1 stick) plus 3 tablespoons butter, melted
1 (6 ounce) box herb-stuffing mix

- Preheat oven to 325°.

- Cook squash, zucchini and bell peppers in salted water for 8 to 10 minutes or until just tender-crisp and drain well. (Do not over cook.) Stir in carrots, chicken soup and sour cream; mix well.

- Melt ½ cup (1 stick) butter in large saucepan and add stuffing mix, mix well and reserve 1 cup for topping. Add vegetable-soup mixture and mix gently, but well.

- Spoon into sprayed 9 x 13-inch baking dish and sprinkle reserved stuffing mix over top.

- Drizzle remaining 3 tablespoons melted butter over top and bake uncovered for 35 minutes. Serves 10.

Make, Bake & Take: Vegetables

A happy heart makes the face cheerful. Proverbs 15:13

Speedy Zucchini and Fettuccine

1 (9 ounce) package refrigerated fresh fettuccine
⅓ cup extra-virgin olive oil, divided
1 tablespoon minced garlic
4 small zucchini, grated
1 tablespoon lemon juice
½ cup pine nuts, toasted
⅓ cup grated parmesan cheese

- Cook fettuccine according to package directions, drain and place in serving bowl.

- Heat large skillet over high heat and add 2 tablespoons oil, garlic and zucchini. Saute for 1 minute.

- Add zucchini mixture to pasta with lemon juice, pine nuts and a little salt and pepper.

- Stir in remaining olive oil and toss to combine. Sprinkle parmesan cheese over top of dish to serve. Serves 8 to 10.

He has made everything beautiful in its time. Ecclesiastes 3:11

Spinach-Artichoke Special

2 (16 ounce) packages frozen chopped spinach, thawed
1 onion, chopped
1 sweet red bell pepper, seeded, chopped
½ cup (1 stick) butter
1 (8 ounce) package cream cheese, cubed
1 teaspoon seasoned salt
1 (14 ounce) can artichokes, drained, chopped
¾ cup shredded parmesan cheese

- Preheat oven to 350°.
- In saucepan, cook spinach according to package directions, drain thoroughly and set aside.
- In skillet saute onion and bell pepper in butter until onion is clear but not browned.
- On low heat add cream cheese and stir constantly until cheese melts. Stir in spinach, salt and artichokes and pour into sprayed 3-quart baking dish.
- Cover and bake for 30 minutes. Uncover, sprinkle parmesan cheese over top of casserole and return to oven for 5 minutes. Serves 10.

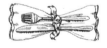

Greater love has no one than this, that he lay down his life for his friends.
John 15:13

Make, Bake & Take: Vegetables

 Super Spinach Bake

¼ cup (½ stick) butter
⅔ cup cracker crumbs
2 (10 ounce) packages frozen chopped spinach, thawed, drained
1 (8 ounce) package shredded cheddar cheese, divided
1 (8 ounce) carton sour cream
1 tablespoon dry onion soup mix

- Preheat oven to 325°.
- Melt butter in skillet over medium heat and add cracker crumbs. Cook, stirring often, for 5 minutes or until crumbs are light brown; set aside.
- In medium bowl, combine spinach, 1 cup cheese, sour cream and soup mix. Spoon into sprayed 7 x 11-inch baking dish. Top with browned crumbs.
- Bake uncovered for 30 minutes. Remove from oven, sprinkle remaining cheese over top and return to oven for 5 minutes. Serves 8.

On the first day of the week we came together to break bread.
Acts 20:7

Spinach-Artichoke Bake

1 (9 inch) frozen piecrust
1 (8 ounce) package cream cheese, softened
1 (14 ounce) jar artichoke hearts, drained, chopped
1 (10 ounce) package frozen chopped spinach, thawed, drained
1 (1.8 ounce) box dry vegetable soup mix
1 (8 ounce) package shredded mozzarella cheese

- Preheat oven to 425°.
- Fit piecrust into 9-inch tart pan with removable bottom. Pierce dough with fork several times and line bottom with foil.
- Fill with dried beans, rice or pie weights (to keep pastry from puffing up). Bake for 15 minutes. Remove foil and weights and bake another 5 minutes.
- In mixing bowl, beat cream cheese until creamy. At low speed add artichokes, spinach, soup mix and half cheese. Spread evenly on crust.
- Sprinkle remaining half cheese over top and bake for 35 minutes or until light brown. Cool 15 minutes before serving and remove sides of pan. Serves 8.

Cast your cares on the Lord and he will sustain you.
Psalm 55:22

Make, Bake & Take: Vegetables

Spinach Enchiladas

2 (10 ounce) boxes chopped spinach, thawed, drained
1 (1 ounce) packet dry onion soup mix
1 (12 ounce) package shredded cheddar cheese, divided
1 (12 ounce) package shredded Monterey Jack cheese, divided
12 flour tortillas
1 pint whipping cream, not whipped

- Preheat oven to 350°.
- Drain spinach well using several paper towels. (Spinach must be well drained.) In medium bowl, combine spinach and onion soup mix and blend in half of both cheeses.
- Spread out 12 tortillas, place about 3 heaping tablespoons spinach mixture down middle of each tortilla and roll.
- Place each filled tortilla, seam-side down, into sprayed 11 x 14-inch baking dish. Pour whipping cream over enchiladas and sprinkle with remaining cheeses.
- Cover and bake for 20 minutes. Remove from oven, remove cover and bake another 10 minutes. Do not over bake. Serves 10 to 12.

But may the righteous be glad and rejoice before God; may they be happy and joyful. Psalm 68:3

Potato-Stuffed Bell Peppers

3 baking potatoes
6 large red bell peppers
Paprika

- Preheat oven at 425°.
- Pierce each potato 3 to 4 times and place on oven rack. Bake for 1 hour 20 to 30 minutes. Cool about 20 minutes.
- While potatoes cook, cut bell peppers in half lengthwise through stem. Remove seed and membranes, rinse and pat dry. Set aside.

Stuffing:
1 (8 ounce) carton sour cream
1 cup shredded colby Jack cheese
¼ cup (½ stick) butter, melted
3 fresh green onions, finely chopped
2 teaspoons dried parsley

- Peel cooked potatoes and mash slightly with potato masher. Add sour cream, cheese, butter, chopped green onion, parsley and a little salt and pepper; mix well.
- Spoon potatoes into bell pepper halves and sprinkle with paprika.
- Bell peppers may be grilled for about 20 minutes or baked at 425° for about 10 to 15 minutes. Serves 6.

A friend loveth at all times. Proverbs 17:17

Vegetables You'll Remember

A retired minister's wife brought this great dish
to a church supper and it was an immediate hit.
We requested it at every supper after then.

2 (15 ounce) cans mixed vegetables, drained
1 cup chopped celery
½ onion, chopped
1 (8 ounce) can sliced water chestnuts, drained
1 cup shredded sharp cheddar cheese
¾ cup mayonnaise
1½ cups round buttery crackers, crushed
6 tablespoons (¾ stick) butter, melted

- Preheat oven to 350°.

- In bowl, combine mixed vegetables, celery, onion, water chestnuts, cheese and mayonnaise and mix well. Spoon into sprayed 3-quart baking dish.

- Combine crushed crackers and melted butter and sprinkle over vegetable mixture.

- Bake for 30 minutes or until crackers are light brown. Serves 8 to 10.

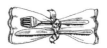

Because of the increase in wickedness, the love of most will grow cold, but he who stands firm to the end will be saved. Matthew 24:12, 13

Hearty Maple Beans

½ pound Polish sausage, thinly sliced
1 onion, very finely chopped
1 (15 ounce) can pork and beans
1 (15 ounce) can pinto beans, drained
1 (15 ounce) can navy beans, drained
¾ cup maple syrup
2 tablespoons vinegar
3 tablespoons ketchup
1 tablespoon mustard
¼ cup bacon bits

- Preheat oven to 350°.
- In large bowl, combine all ingredients except bacon bits and stir to blend well.
- Pour into 3-quart baking dish and bake uncovered for 25 minutes. Remove from oven, sprinkle bacon bits over top and return to oven for 5 minutes. Serves 10 to 12.

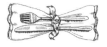

For God so loved the world that he gave his one and only Son, that whoever believes in him shall not perish but have eternal life. John 3:16

Black-Eyed Peas and Ham

This is a great dish for leftover or deli ham.

3 (15 ounce) cans black-eyed peas with liquid
1½ cups coarsely chopped ham
1 onion, chopped
1 pound small, fresh whole okra pods

- In large saucepan, combine peas, ham and onion and bring to a boil, reduce heat and simmer 10 minutes.
- Place all okra on top of peas-ham mixture, cover and cook on medium heat about 10 minutes or until okra is tender. When serving, remove okra with slotted spoon to plate. Pour peas into serving bowl and place okra on top of peas. Serves 8 to 10.

Lucky Black-Eyed Peas

2 (10 ounce) packages frozen black-eyed peas
¼ cup (½ stick) butter
1 large green bell pepper, seeded, chopped
1 small onion, chopped
1 (15 ounce) can Mexican stewed tomatoes with liquid

- Cook black-eyed peas according to package directions and drain. In large skillet melt butter and saute bell pepper and onion.
- Stir in black-eyed peas, stewed tomatoes and a little salt and pepper. Bring to a boil, reduce heat and simmer 10 minutes or until most of liquid cooks out; stir often. Serves 8 to 10.

The fool says in his heart, "There is no God." Psalm 14:1

Southern Hoppin' John

*Hoppin' John is a beloved southern comfort food and is considered
"lucky", especially when served on New Year's Day.*

1 pound bulk sausage
1 (16 ounce) package frozen chopped onion and bell peppers
1 (14 ounce) can chicken broth
1¼ cups instant white rice
1 teaspoon minced garlic
2 (15 ounce) cans black-eyed peas

- In large pot, brown and cook sausage, onions and bell
  peppers over medium-high heat.

- Drain and add chicken broth, rice, garlic and a little salt
  and pepper. Bring to a boil, reduce heat and simmer 15
  minutes, stirring occasionally.

- Drain, rinse peas and add to pot. Simmer for additional
  10 minutes or until liquid absorbs. Serves 6 to 8.

Supreme Mashed Potatoes

1 (8 ounce) package cream cheese, softened
½ cup sour cream
2 tablespoons butter, softened
1 (1 ounce) packet ranch salad dressing mix
8 cups warm instant mashed potatoes

- Preheat oven to 350°.

- In mixing bowl, combine cream cheese, sour cream,
  butter and ranch salad dressing mix; beat until smooth.
  Stir in warm potatoes and mix well.

- Transfer to sprayed 3-quart baking dish, cover and
  bake for 25 minutes or until mixture is thoroughly hot.
  Serves 8.

Whipped Potato Bake

4 pounds potatoes, peeled, cubed
½ cup (1 stick) butter, softened
1 (8 ounce) carton whipping cream
1 (8 ounce) carton cream cheese with chives
1½ teaspoons garlic salt
1 cup slivered almonds

- Preheat oven to 350°.
- Place potatoes and a little salt in large saucepan and cover with water. Bring to a boil, reduce heat and cook about 15 minutes or until potatoes are tender. Drain.
- With mixer, beat potatoes until smooth and add butter, whipping cream, cream cheese and garlic salt.
- Beat until butter melts and mixture blends well.
- Pour into sprayed 9 x 13-inch baking dish and bake uncovered for 20 minutes.
- Remove from oven and sprinkle almonds over top of casserole.
- Bake uncovered for additional 20 minutes or until potatoes are light brown. Serves 10 to 12.

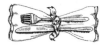

Study to show thyself approved unto God. Second Timothy 2:15

The Perfect Potato

4 large baking potatoes, baked

Stuffing:
4 tablespoons (½ stick) butter
4 tablespoons sour cream
1 cup finely chopped ham
1 (10 ounce) package frozen broccoli florets, coarsely chopped
1 cup shredded sharp cheddar cheese

- Preheat oven to 400°.

- Slit potatoes down center, but not through to bottom. For each potato, use 1 tablespoon each of butter and sour cream. With fork, work in ¼ cup ham, ¼ broccoli and ¼ cup cheese.

- Just before serving, place potatoes on baking sheet and heat for 10 minutes. Serves 4.

Creamy Ranch Potatoes

4 medium russet potatoes, peeled, quartered
¼ cup (½ stick) butter
⅓ cup ranch salad dressing
2 tablespoons, cooked, crumbled bacon

- In saucepan, boil potatoes in water about 15 minutes or until tender. Drain and beat potatoes with electric mixer until smooth.

- Add butter, ½ teaspoon salt and a little black pepper and beat until butter melts. Gradually add salad dressing; beat until smooth. Spoon into serving bowl and top with crumbled bacon. Serves 8.

Baked Potato Supper

4 large baking potatoes, baked
1½ cups diced ham
1 (10 ounce) can cream of broccoli soup
¼ cup milk
½ cup shredded cheddar cheese

- Preheat oven to 375°.

- Cut baked potatoes in half lengthwise, scoop out meat of potato and leave about ¼-inch on skin. Coarsely mash potatoes with fork.

- In saucepan heat ham, soup and milk; stir just until soup and milk mix. Stir in mashed potatoes, ham and a little salt and pepper and mix well.

- Spoon mixture into potato skins, top with shredded cheese and bake for 5 to 10 minutes. Serve while potatoes are steamy hot. Serves 4.

Sweet Potato Bake

2 (15 ounce) cans sweet potatoes, drained, divided
1½ cups packed brown sugar
¼ cup (½ stick) butter, melted
¾ cup chopped pecans
1 cup miniature marshmallows

- Preheat oven to 350°.

- Place can sweet potatoes in sprayed 2-quart baking dish.

- In bowl, combine brown sugar, butter and pecans and sprinkle half of this mixture over sweet potatoes. Make second layer of sweet potatoes and brown sugar mixture, cover and bake for 25 minutes.

- Sprinkle marshmallows on top of potatoes and return to oven for 10 to 15 minutes or until marshmallows are light brown. Serves 8 to 10.

Sweet Potato-Pineapple Bake

2 (15 ounce) cans sweet potatoes, drained
1 (8 ounce) can crushed pineapple with juice
3 tablespoons butter, melted
⅔ cup chopped pecans
¾ cup packed brown sugar
½ teaspoon cinnamon
1½ cups miniature marshmallows, divided

- Preheat oven to 350°.

- In bowl, lightly mash sweet potatoes with fork and stir in pineapple, butter, pecans, brown sugar, cinnamon and pinch of salt.

- Stir in half the marshmallows and mix well. Transfer to sprayed 2-quart baking dish. Cover and bake 25 minutes.

- Remove casserole from oven and spread remaining marshmallows over top of sweet potato mixture.

- Return to oven and bake for 10 to 15 minutes or until marshmallows are slightly puffed and light brown. Serves 8 to 10.

Great are the works of the Lord; they are pondered by all who delight in them. Psalm 111:2

Make, Bake & Take: Side Dishes

Sweet Potato Casserole

2 (15 ounce) cans sweet potatoes, drained
½ cup applesauce
1 cup Craisins®
½ cup chopped walnuts or pecans

- Preheat oven to 350°.
- Mash sweet potatoes, but leave them slightly chunky. Combine applesauce, Craisins® and chopped nuts; mix well. Transfer to sprayed 3-quart baking dish.

Sauce:
1 cup packed brown sugar
¼ cup (½ stick) butter
½ cup peach or apricot preserves

- In saucepan, combine brown sugar, butter and preserves and heat just enough to be able to mix well. Spoon over sweet potato mixture, cover and bake for 30 minutes. Serves 8.

A Different Macaroni

1 (8 ounce) package shell macaroni
½ cup whipping cream
1 (8 ounce) carton shredded gorgonzola cheese
1 (10 ounce) package frozen green peas, thawed
2 cups cubed ham

- Cook macaroni according to package directions and drain. Add cream and gorgonzola cheese and stir until cheese melts.
- Fold in peas and ham and cook on low heat, stirring constantly, 5 minutes or until mixture is thoroughly hot. Spoon into serving bowl and serve hot. Serves 10.

Worth-It Macaroni

2 cups macaroni
2 cups milk
¼ cup flour
1 (12 ounce) package shredded sharp cheddar cheese
1 cup soft breadcrumbs
¼ cup (½ stick) butter, melted

- Preheat oven to 350°.

- Cook macaroni according to package directions, drain and set aside. In jar with lid, combine milk, flour and an ample amount of seasoned salt; shake to mix well.

- In large bowl, combine macaroni, flour-milk mixture and cheese. Pour into sprayed 9 x 13-inch baking dish. Stir melted butter over breadcrumbs, toss and sprinkle over top.

- Cover and bake for 35 minutes, remove cover and return to oven for 10 minutes. Serves 8.

Macaroni and Cheese Deluxe

1 (8 ounce) package small shell macaroni
3 tablespoons butter, melted
1 (15 ounce) can stewed tomatoes
1 (8 ounce) package shredded Velveeta® cheese
1 cup crushed potato chips, optional

- Preheat oven to 350°.

- Cook macaroni according to package directions, drain and place in bowl. While macaroni is still hot, stir in butter, tomatoes, cheese and a little salt and pepper and mix well.

- Pour into sprayed 2-quart baking dish, cover and bake for 25 minutes. Remove from oven, uncover and sprinkle with crushed potato chips. Bake another 10 minutes or until potato chips are light brown. Serves 8.

 Spice Up The Macaroni

Macaroni:

1 (8 ounce) package spiral pasta
⅓ cup butter

- Cook macaroni according to package directions, drain and add butter, stir until butter melts. Cover, set aside and keep warm.

Spicy Tomatoes:

1 (8 ounce) package shredded Mexican Velveeta® cheese
1 (10 ounce) can tomatoes and green chilies with liquid
½ yellow onion, finely diced
1 (8 ounce) carton sour cream

- Preheat oven to 325°.
- In large saucepan, combine cheese, tomatoes and green chilies and diced onion. Stir in macaroni, heat on low for 5 minutes and stir occasionally.
- Fold in sour cream and pour into 2-quart baking dish. Cover and bake for 20 minutes. Serves 8.

Live in peace with each other. First Thessalonians 5:13

Make, Bake & Take: Side Dishes

Cheesy Noodle Casserole

1 (8 ounce) package egg noodles
1 (16 ounce) package frozen broccoli florets, thawed
1 sweet red bell pepper, seeded, chopped
1 (8 ounce) package shredded Velveeta® cheese
1 cup milk
¾ cup coarsely crushed bite-size cheese crackers

- Preheat oven to 350°.

- Cook noodles in large saucepan according to package directions. Add broccoli and bell pepper for last 2 minutes of cooking time. Drain in colander.

- In same saucepan, combine cheese and milk over low heat and stir until cheese melts. Stir in noodle-broccoli mixture and spoon into sprayed 3-quart baking dish.

- Sprinkle with crushed crackers and bake uncovered for 25 to 30 minutes or until top is golden brown. Serves 10.

Couscous and Veggies

1 (6 ounce) box herbed chicken-flavored couscous
¼ cup (½ stick) butter
1 red bell pepper, seeded, chopped
1 medium yellow squash, seeded, cubed
1 cup broccoli florets, coarsely chopped

- Preheat oven to 325°.

- Cook couscous according to package directions, but omit butter. Melt butter in saucepan and saute bell pepper, squash and broccoli. Cook about 10 minutes.

- Combine couscous and vegetables and add a little salt and pepper. Spoon into sprayed 2-quart baking dish.

- Cover and bake about 15 minutes or just until mixture is thoroughly hot. Serves 8.

Artichoke Fettuccine

1 (12 ounce) package fettuccine
1 (14 ounce) can water-packed artichoke hearts, drained, chopped
1 (10 ounce) box frozen green peas, thawed
1 (16 ounce) jar alfredo sauce
2 heaping tablespoons crumbled blue cheese

- Cook fettuccine according to package directions. Drain and place in serving bowl to keep warm.

- In large saucepan, heat artichoke hearts, peas and alfredo sauce. Stir well, spoon into bowl with fettuccine and toss. Sprinkle with blue cheese and serve hot. Serves 10.

Italian-Style Rice and Beans

1 (16 ounce) package frozen chopped onions and bell peppers
2 tablespoons olive oil
1 (15 ounce) can Italian stewed tomatoes
1 (15 ounce) can great northern beans, drained
1 cup instant rice

- In large saucepan, saute onions and bell peppers in oil. Add stewed tomatoes, beans, ½ cup water and rice and stir well.

- Over medium-high heat, cover and cook about 3 minutes. Uncover and continue cooking another 3 minutes, stirring once, or until rice is tender. Serves 8.

… let every man be swift to hear, slow to speak, slow to wrath.
James 1:19

Supper Frittata

2 cups cooked white rice
1 (10 ounce) box frozen green peas, thawed
1 cup cooked, cubed ham
8 large eggs, beaten
1 cup shredded pepper Jack cheese, divided
1 teaspoon dried thyme

- In large, ovenproof, heavy skillet with a little oil, heat rice, peas and ham 3 to 4 minutes or until mixture is thoroughly hot.
- In separate bowl, whisk eggs, three-fourths of cheese, thyme and a little salt.
- Add to mixture in skillet and shake pan gently to distribute evenly.
- On medium heat, cover and cook, without stirring, until set on bottom and sides. (Eggs will still be runny in center.)
- Sprinkle remaining cheese over top. Place ovenproof skillet in oven and broil about 5 minutes or until frittata is firm in center. Serves 8 to 10.

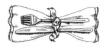

In God I have put my trust: I will not be afraid what man can do unto me. Psalm 56:11

Parmesan-Garlic Orzo

1 (10 ounce) box original plain couscous
3 teaspoons minced garlic
¼ cup olive oil
½ cup grated parmesan cheese
¼ cup milk
1 tablespoon dried parsley
1 (8 ounce) can green peas, drained

- In large saucepan, bring 2 cups water to a boil, stir in couscous and cover. Let stand 5 minutes. Stir in garlic, oil, parmesan cheese, milk, parsley, peas and a little salt and pepper.

- Cook and stir until thoroughly hot. Serves 8.

TIP: You might want to garnish with 3 fresh, sliced green onions.

Ranch Spaghetti

1 (12 ounce) package spaghetti
¼ cup (½ stick) butter, cut in 3 pieces
¾ cup sour cream
¾ cup bottled ranch dressing
½ cup grated parmesan cheese

- Cook spaghetti according to package directions, drain and return to saucepan. Stir in butter, sour cream and ranch dressing and toss.

- Spoon into serving bowl and sprinkle with grated parmesan cheese. Serves 8.

TIP: You can make a main dish with this recipe just by adding 1 or 2 cups cubed ham or turkey.

Pecan-Mushroom Rice

1 cup whole pecans
1½ cups instant rice
2 cups chicken broth
2 tablespoons butter
2 (8 ounce) cans whole mushrooms, drained
2 teaspoons minced garlic
3 cups baby spinach leaves without stems
½ cup grated parmesan cheese

- In large saucepan, cook and stir pecans over medium heat for 5 minutes. Remove from pan and cool slightly.
- Cook rice in chicken broth and butter according to package directions. Gently stir in mushrooms, garlic, spinach, parmesan cheese and pecans. Serves 8.

Cheesy Grits Bake

¼ cup (½ stick) butter
3½ cups milk, divided
1⅓ cups quick-cooking grits
1 (8 ounce) package shredded Monterey Jack cheese
5 large eggs, beaten
1 teaspoon hot sauce

- Preheat oven to 325°.
- In large saucepan, bring butter, a little salt and 1½ cups milk, to a boil. Stir constantly and add grits. Reduce heat and simmer for 5 minutes. Stir in cheese.
- In large bowl, whisk eggs, hot sauce and remaining 2 cups milk until they blend well. Gradually stir in grits and pour into sprayed 3-quart baking dish.
- Bake uncovered for 45 minutes or until knife inserted in center comes out clean. Serves 10.

 Caramel-Coconut Cake

1 (18 ounce) package white cake mix with pudding
3 large eggs
⅓ cup oil
2 cups flaked coconut, divided

- Preheat oven to 350°.
- In mixing bowl, combine cake mix, eggs, oil and 1¼ cups water and beat on low speed for 1 minute; then beat on high speed for 2 minutes.
- Stir in ¾ cup coconut and pour into sprayed, floured 9 x 13-inch baking pan.
- Bake for 30 minutes or until toothpick inserted in center comes out clean.

Topping:
½ cup (1 stick) butter
⅔ cup caramel ice cream topping
4 tablespoons milk
1 cup chopped pecans
1 (6 ounce) package butterscotch chips

- While cake is baking, prepare topping. In saucepan on medium heat, melt butter and stir in caramel topping and milk.
- Boil for 5 to 6 minutes or until thick and it reaches spreading consistency; stir constantly.
- Stir in pecans and remaining coconut and spread over cake immediately after it comes out of oven. Sprinkle butterscotch chips over top and cool completely before cutting into squares. Serves 12 to 14.

Nutmeg Cake

2 cups flour
1 teaspoon baking powder
1 teaspoon ground nutmeg
½ teaspoon baking soda
¼ cup (½ stick) butter, softened
¼ cup shortening
1½ cups sugar
½ teaspoon vanilla
3 eggs
1 cup buttermilk
1 (16 ounce) can lemon icing

- Preheat oven to 350.
- Combine flour, baking powder, nutmeg, baking soda and a little salt; set aside.
- In mixing bowl beat butter and shortening, add sugar and vanilla and beat until they mix well. Add eggs, one at a time, and beat well after each addition.
- Alternately add flour mixture and buttermilk and beat on low speed after each addition until they mix well.
- Spread batter into sprayed 9 x 13-inch baking pan and bake for 30 to 35 minutes or until toothpick inserted near center comes out clean. Cool on wire rack and spread with lemon icing.

Live as servants of God. First Peter 2:16

Lemon Poppy Seed Cake

1 (18 ounce) box lemon pudding cake mix
1 (8 ounce) carton sour cream
3 eggs
⅓ cup oil
2 tablespoons poppy seeds
Powdered sugar for topping

- Preheat oven to 350°.
- Spray and flour bundt pan. Combine cake mix, sour cream, eggs, oil and ¼ cup water in mixing bowl and beat on medium speed until it mixes well.
- Stir in poppy seeds and mix until seeds are evenly distributed.
- Pour batter into bundt pan and bake for 45 minutes or until toothpick inserted in center comes out clean.
- Dust with powdered sugar or use part of 1 (16 ounce) can vanilla icing. Serves 16.

As arrows are in the hand of a mighty man: so are children of the youth. Happy is the man that hath quiver full of them. Psalm 127:4, 5

Chocolate-Pecan Chess Pie

This pie is absolutely ultra-decadent and delicious.
It is so rich you can even cut pieces a little smaller than usual.

1 (9 inch) frozen unbaked piecrust
1⅓ cups sugar
1 tablespoon cornmeal
4 eggs, beaten
⅓ cup half-and-half cream
¼ cup (½ stick) butter, melted
1 teaspoon vanilla
⅔ cup chopped pecans
½ cup miniature semi-sweet chocolate chips

- Preheat oven to 425°.
- Roll out piecrust according to package directions and place in 9-inch pie plate.
- Trim pastry ½-inch beyond edge of pie plate and fold under extra pastry. Flute edge high around pie plate. Bake for 8 minutes. Reduce heat to 325°.
- For filling, combine sugar and cornmeal. Stir in eggs, mix well and gradually stir in cream, melted butter and vanilla. Add pecans.
- Sprinkle chocolate chips over bottom of pastry and carefully pour filling into piecrust over chocolate chips.
- To prevent crust from getting too brown, cut 1-inch strip of foil and cover pastry edges.
- Bake for 40 to 45 minutes or until center appears set. Cool; refrigerate pie until time to take to church. Serves 6 to 8.

Make, Bake & Take: Pies

Do not let your hearts be troubled. Trust in God. John 14:1

Creamy Pumpkin Pie

1 (6 serving) instant vanilla pudding mix
½ cup milk
½ cup sugar
1 teaspoon pumpkin-pie spice
1 cup canned pumpkin
1 (8 ounce) carton whipped topping, thawed
1 (9 inch) graham cracker piecrust

- In large bowl, combine instant pudding, milk, sugar and pumpkin pie spice; beat or whisk 1 minute (mixture will be very thick). Stir in pumpkin, fold in whipped topping and blend well.
- Spoon into piecrust and spread evenly over crust. Refrigerate at least 3 hours before slicing to serve.
- Store in refrigerator until ready to leave for church supper. Serves 6 to 8.

Let love and faithfulness never leave you; bind them around your neck, write them on the tablet of your heart. Proverbs 3:3

Chocolate-Caramel Pie

1 (9 inch) prepared chocolate-crumb piecrust
½ cup chopped pecans
18 squares individually wrapped caramels
¼ cup canned evaporated milk
1 (8 ounce) package semi-sweet chocolate chips
1 (8 ounce) carton whipping cream
3 tablespoons butter

- Sprinkle pecans over prepared piecrust. In heavy saucepan on low heat, melt caramels and evaporated milk and stir often until mixture is smooth. Pour caramel mixture over pecans.

- Heat chocolate chips, cream and butter in heavy saucepan and stir until mixture is smooth. Pour over caramel layer and refrigerate at least 4 hours before serving. Serves 6 to 8.

Luscious Strawberry Pie

1 (24 ounce) package frozen, sweetened strawberries, thawed
4 tablespoons cornstarch
1 (9 inch) ready shortbread piecrust
1½ cups whipping cream
⅓ cup powdered sugar

- In saucepan, stir together strawberries, ¼ cup water and cornstarch. Stir constantly over medium heat until mixture boils.

- Continue cooking and stir until mixture is thick. Remove from heat, cool 20 minutes and spoon into crust. Refrigerate 2 to 4 hours.

- In mixing bowl, beat whipping cream and powdered sugar until stiff peaks form. Spread over strawberry mixture. Refrigerate. Serves 6 to 8.

Thanksgiving Pie

1 (15 ounce) can pumpkin
1 cup sugar
2 eggs, beaten
1½ teaspoons pumpkin pie spice
1 (12 ounce) can evaporated milk
1 (9 inch) unbaked piecrust

- Preheat oven to 425°.
- In bowl, combine pumpkin, sugar, beaten eggs, pumpkin pie spice, evaporated milk and a pinch of salt and mix well. Pour into unbaked piecrust and bake for 15 minutes.
- Reduce oven heat to 325° and continue baking another 50 minutes or until knife inserted in center comes out clean. Serves 8.

Those that be planted in the house of the Lord shall flourish in the courts of our God. Psalm 92:13

Blueberry Cobbler

1 (20 ounce) can blueberry pie filling
½ cup sugar
1 tablespoon lemon juice

- Combine blueberry pie filling, sugar and lemon juice and stir to blend. Spoon into sprayed 9-inch square baking dish.

Pastry:
1½ cups biscuit mix
¼ cup plus 1 tablespoon sugar
¼ cup (½ stick) butter, divided
¾ cup sour cream

- In large bowl, combine biscuit mix and ¼ cup sugar and cut in three-fourths butter until mixture is crumbly.
- Stir in sour cream; toss with fork until mixture forms a ball.
- Roll out to fit top of baking dish and place pastry over filling. Melt remaining butter and brush over pastry. Sprinkle 1 tablespoon sugar over top. Serves 6 to 8.

Neither height nor depth, nor anything else in all creation, will be able to separate us from the love of God. Romans 8:39

Apple Crumble

1 (20 ounce) can apple pie filling
½ cup packed brown sugar
½ teaspoon ground cinnamon
½ teaspoon ground ginger

- Preheat oven to 350°.
- In bowl, combine apple pie filling, ½ cup brown sugar, cinnamon and ginger. Spoon into sprayed 9-inch square baking dish.

Topping:
1 cup flour
¾ cup packed brown sugar
¼ teaspoon cinnamon
½ cup (1 stick) butter
⅓ cup slivered almonds

- In bowl, combine flour, ¾ cup brown sugar and remaining cinnamon.
- Cut in butter until mixture resembles coarse crumbs. Add almonds and sprinkle over apple mixture.
- Bake for 35 to 40 minutes or until filling is bubbly and topping is golden brown. Serves 6 to 8.

Trust in the Lord and do good. Psalm 37:3

4-Ingredient Fast Fixes

I ncludes 76 fast, easy 4-ingredient dishes to get you to the church on time! ... Favorites for last-minute and hurry-up covered dishes.

Main Dishes.. 172

Vegetables, Sides and Breads 190

Salads 202

Desserts... 208

Cheesy Crusted Chicken

¾ cup mayonnaise (not light)
½ cup grated parmesan cheese
5 boneless, skinless chicken breast halves
1 cup Italian seasoned dry breadcrumbs

- Preheat oven to 400°.
- Combine mayonnaise and cheese. Place chicken breasts on sheet of wax paper and spread mayonnaise-cheese mixture over chicken. Sprinkle heavily with dry bread-crumbs, turn breasts over and sprinkle other side heav-ily with breadcrumbs.
- Place chicken on large sprayed baking pan with pieces not touching each other. Bake for 20 minutes (25 minutes if chicken pieces are fairly large). Chicken pieces may be sliced and placed on serving platter. Serves 5.

Cranberry Chicken

2 small chickens, quartered
1 (1 ounce) package dry onion soup mix
1 (16 ounce) can whole cranberry sauce
1 (8 ounce) bottle sweet-honey Catalina salad dressing

- Preheat oven to 375°.
- Dry chicken quarters and place in single layer in sprayed 11 x 14-inch baking pan.
- In saucepan over medium heat, combine soup mix, cran-berry sauce and dressing. Heat, while stirring, just until ingredients blend well and spoon over chicken quarters.
- Cover with foil and bake for 35 minutes. Remove foil, reduce heat to 325° and bake an additional 25 minutes. Serves 8.

Creamy Chicken and Broccoli

5 large boneless, skinless chicken breast halves
2 (10 ounce) cans creamy chicken verde
½ cup milk
1 (16 ounce) package frozen broccoli florets, thawed

- In very large skillet (with lid) sprinkle chicken with a little salt and pepper and brown breasts in a little oil. On medium-high heat, stir into skillet both cans of soup and milk. Stir to mix and spoon soup mixture over top of chicken breasts. When mixture mixes well and is hot, reduce heat to low, cover and simmer for 20 minutes.

- Place broccoli florets around chicken in creamy sauce. Return heat to high until broccoli is hot; then reduce heat and simmer about 10 minutes or until broccoli is tender-crisp.

- Serve chicken and sauce over hot brown rice. Serves 5.

Crispy Nutty Chicken Breasts

5 - 6 boneless, skinless chicken breast halves
1 (8 ounce) bottle Catalina dressing
½ cup finely chopped pecans
2 cups crushed buttery cracker crumbs

- Marinate chicken breasts in Catalina dressing for 3 to 4 hours. Discard marinade.

- Preheat oven to 350°.

- Combine pecans and crumbs and place in shallow bowl. Dip each chicken breast in pecan-crumb mixture and place in sprayed 9 x 13-inch baking pan.

- Bake, uncovered, for 35 to 40 minutes or until chicken is light brown. Serves 5 to 6.

Crunchy Chicken Breasts

4 - 5 boneless, skinless chicken breast halves
½ cup Italian salad dressing
½ cup sour cream
2½ cups crushed corn flakes

- Preheat oven to 350°.
- Place chicken in resealable plastic bag, add salad dressing and sour cream. Seal and chill 1 hour.
- Remove chicken from marinade and discard marinade. Dredge chicken in corn flakes and place in sprayed 9 x 13-inch baking dish.
- Bake uncovered for 30 to 35 minutes or until chicken is light brown. Serves 4 to 5.

Saucy Chicken

5 - 6 boneless, skinless chicken breast halves
2 cups thick-and-chunky salsa
⅓ cup packed light brown sugar
1½ tablespoons dijon-style mustard

- Preheat oven to 350°.
- Place chicken breasts in sprayed 9 x 13-inch baking dish.
- Combine salsa, sugar and mustard and pour over chicken.
- Cover and bake for 45 minutes. Serve over rice. Serves 6.

Let love and faithfulness never leave you; bind them around your neck; write them on the tablet of your heart. Proverbs 3:3

Mozzarella Chicken Breasts

1½ cups spaghetti sauce
1½ cups Italian seasoned dry breadcrumbs
6 boneless, skinless chicken breast halves
6 slices mozzarella cheese

- Preheat oven to 325°.
- Pour spaghetti sauce into sprayed 9 x 13-inch baking pan.
- Fill shallow bowl with breadcrumbs, dip each chicken breast in crumbs and press down to coat well. Place chicken breast in spaghetti sauce-filled pan.
- Top each chicken breast with slice of cheese and bake uncovered for 45 minutes. When serving, spoon 1 or 2 tablespoons sauce over each chicken breast. Serves 6.

Mushroom-Onion Chicken

5 - 6 boneless, skinless chicken breast halves
1 (10 ounce) can cream of mushroom soup
1 (10 ounce) can cream of onion soup
1 cup cooking wine

- Preheat oven to 325°.
- In sprayed skillet on medium-high heat, brown chicken breasts. Place in sprayed 9 x 13-inch baking pan.
- Combine mushroom soup, onion soup and cooking wine; pour over chicken breasts. Cover and bake 25 minutes. Uncover chicken and bake another 25 minutes. Serves 5

Great is the Lord and most worthy of praise. Psalm 48:1

Parmesan Chicken

1 (1 ounce) packet dry Italian salad dressing mix
½ cup grated parmesan cheese
¼ cup flour
5 boneless, skinless chicken breast halves

- Preheat oven to 375°.
- In shallow bowl, combine salad dressing mix, cheese and flour. Moisten chicken with a little water and coat with cheese mixture. Place in sprayed 9 x 13-inch baking pan.
- Bake for 30 to 35 minutes or until chicken is light brown and it cooks thoroughly. Serves 5.

Requested Favorite Chicken

6 boneless, skinless chicken breast halves
1 (16 ounce) jar thick-and-chunky hot salsa
1 cup packed light brown sugar
1 tablespoon dijon-style mustard

- Preheat oven to 325°.
- In large skillet with a little oil, brown chicken breasts and place in sprayed 9 x 13-inch baking dish.
- Combine salsa, brown sugar, mustard and ½ teaspoon salt and pour over chicken. Cover and bake for 45 minutes. Serve over hot, cooked brown rice. Serves 6.

Sin shall not be your master, because you are not under law, you are under grace. Romans 6:24

Supper-Ready Limeade Chicken

6 large boneless, skinless chicken breast halves
1 (6 ounce) can frozen limeade concentrate, thawed
3 tablespoons brown sugar
½ cup chili sauce

- Sprinkle chicken breasts with a little salt and pepper and place in sprayed skillet over high heat. Cook and brown on both sides for about 10 minutes. Remove from skillet and set aside to keep warm.

- Add limeade concentrate, brown sugar and chili sauce to skillet and bring to a boil. Cook, stirring constantly, for 4 minutes. Return chicken to skillet and spoon sauce over chicken.

- Reduce heat, cover and simmer for 15 minutes. Serve over hot, buttered rice. Serves 4.

Sweet-Spicy Chicken Thighs

3 tablespoons chili powder
3 tablespoons honey
2 tablespoons lemon juice
8 - 10 chicken thighs

- Preheat oven to 425°.

- Line 10 x 15-inch shallow baking pan with heavy foil and set metal rack on top. Combine chili powder, honey, lemon juice and a lot of salt and pepper.

- Brush mixture over chicken thighs, place on rack and turn thighs to coat completely. Bake for about 35 minutes and turn over once. Serves 6.

Rejoice with me; I have found my lost sheep. Luke 15:6

Turkey and the Works

1 (6 ounce) stuffing mix for turkey
½ (16 ounce) can whole cranberry sauce
1 pound turkey tenderloin, sliced thin
1 (12 ounce) jar turkey gravy

- Preheat oven to 325°.

- Prepare stuffing mix according to package directions. You will need ¼ cup (½ stick) butter. Measure 1 cup cranberry sauce and stir into prepared stuffing mix.

- In skillet with a little oil, brown turkey slices and simmer, covered, for about 10 minutes or until liquid evaporates.

- Place turkey slices in sprayed 7 x 11-inch baking dish. Cover with turkey gravy and spoon prepared stuffing mix over turkey and gravy. Cover and bake for 25 minutes. Serves 8.

TIP: To use remaining half can of cranberry sauce, add 1 (8 ounce) can crushed pineapple, ¾ cup apricot or peach preserves and ½ cup chopped pecans. You will have a delightful cranberry relish that compliments chicken, pork chops, pork roast or thick slices of ham.

He that is without sin among you, let him first cast a stone at her.
John 8:7

Tempting Chicken

3 boneless, skinless chicken breast halves
3 boneless, skinless chicken thighs
1 (16 ounce) jar tomato-alfredo sauce
1 (10 ounce) can tomato-bisque soup

- In large skillet, brown chicken pieces in little oil.
- Pour tomato-alfredo sauce, tomato-bisque soup and ½ cup water over chicken pieces.
- Cover and simmer about 30 minutes. Serves 6.

Roasted Chicken

1 (2½ - 3 pound) whole chicken
2 ribs celery
1 small onion
Oil

- Preheat oven to 325°.
- Rinse chicken and dry with paper towels. Cut celery in half and insert with whole onion into chicken cavity. Tie legs together, rub chicken with a little oil and sprinkle with salt and pepper.
- Place chicken in open roasting pan and cook 20 to 30 minutes per pound or until juices run clear. Baste every 30 minutes with pan juices. (This will make chicken moist and juicy.) Remove onion and celery when ready to serve. Serves 6.

4 Ingredient Main Dishes: Chicken

Smothered Steak

1 large round steak
1 (10 ounce) can golden mushroom soup
1 (1 ounce) packet dry onion soup mix
⅔ cup milk

- Preheat oven to 325°.
- Cut steak into serving-size pieces and place in sprayed 9 x 13-inch baking pan.
- In saucepan, mix soup, onion soup mix and milk. Heat just enough to mix well. Pour over steak.
- Seal with foil. Bake for 1 hour. Serves 6.

Beef-Onion Casserole

2 pounds lean ground beef
1 (1 ounce) packet onion soup mix
1 (10 ounce) can French onion soup
1½ cups instant brown rice

- Preheat oven to 350°.
- Brown beef in large skillet and stir in onion soup mix. Stir in French onion soup, brown rice and 1 cup water and spoon into sprayed 9 x 13-inch baking pan.
- Cover and bake 45 minutes. Serves 8.

All hard work brings a profit, but mere talk leads only to poverty.
Proverbs 14:23

Barbecue Pizza

1 (12 inch) prepared pizza crust
1 (12 ounce) package Mexican shredded cheese, divided
1 pound cooked, shredded barbecue beef
1 (4 ounce) sliced ripe olives, drained

- Preheat oven to 400°.

- Place pizza crust on baking sheet and sprinkle on half of cheese. Spread shredded barbecue over top and sprinkle remaining cheese over barbecue. Arrange olives over top of pizza.

- Bake for 10 minutes or until hot and bubbly. Serves 4.

Creamy Onion-Beef Patties

1½ pounds lean ground beef
½ cup salsa
½ cup butter cracker crumbs
1 (10 ounce) can cream of onion soup

- Combine beef, salsa and cracker crumbs and form into 5 or 6 patties. Brown in skillet, reduce heat, add ½ cup water and simmer 15 minutes.

- In saucepan over medium heat, combine onion soup and ½ cup water; mix well. Pour over patties and simmer about 10 minutes. Serves 5 to 6.

Boast not thyself of tomorrow: for thou knowest not what a day may bring forth. Proverbs 27:1

Quick Skillet Supper

1½ pounds lean ground beef
⅔ cup stir-fry sauce
1 (16 ounce) package frozen stir-fry vegetables
2 (3 ounce) packages Oriental-flavor ramen noodles

- Brown and crumble ground beef in large skillet. Add 2⅓ cups water, stir-fry sauce, vegetables and both seasoning packets contained in noodle package.
- Cook and stir on medium heat about 5 minutes
- Break up noodles, add to beef-vegetable mixture and cook about 6 minutes. Stir to separate noodles as they soften. Serve hot. Serves 4 to 6.

Sirloin in Rich Mushroom Sauce

1 pound boneless beef sirloin, cut in strips
1 (14 ounce) can beef broth
1 (8 ounce) can sliced mushrooms
1 (10 ounce) can cream of mushroom soup

- Brown steak strips in large non-stick skillet with 2 tablespoons oil over medium-high heat. (Sirloin will be tender in less cooking time than cheaper cuts of meat.)
- Add beef broth, a generous amount of pepper and ½ soup can water. Heat to boiling, reduce heat and simmer 15 minutes.
- Spoon mushroom soup, mushrooms and 1 cup water in saucepan and heat just enough to mix well. Pour over steak and simmer 5 minutes. Serve over angel hair pasta. Serves 6.

Speedy Steak Strombolis

1 (2 pound) package frozen pizza dough, thawed
⅔ cup hot salsa
½ pound sliced roast beef
1 (8 ounce) package shredded cheddar cheese

- Preheat oven to 425°.

- On floured work surface, roll out half dough into 10 x 14-inch rectangle.

- Spread half of salsa over dough and leave ½-inch border. Cover with half sliced roast beef and half cheese. Starting at long side, roll jellyroll style, pinching ends together. Place on sprayed baking sheet.

- Repeat with remaining ingredients for second roll. Bake for 20 minutes or until light brown. Cool about 20 minutes and slice to serve. Serves 8.

Thai Beef, Noodles and Veggies

2 (4.4 ounce) packages Thai sesame noodles
1 pound sirloin steak, cut in strips
1 (16 ounce) package frozen stir-fry vegetables, thawed
½ cup chopped peanuts

- Cook noodles according to package directions. Remove from heat, drain and cover. In large skillet with a little oil, season sirloin strips with a little salt and pepper. Add half to skillet, brown and cook 2 minutes and remove to separate bowl. Cook remaining steak and remove to bowl.

- In same skillet place vegetables and ½ cup water, cover and cook 5 minutes or until tender-crisp. Remove from heat. Add steak strips, noodles and vegetables to bowl and toss to mix. To serve, sprinkle with chopped peanuts. Serves 6 to 8.

4 Ingredient Main Dishes: Beef

Sweet Peach Pork Tenderloin

3 tablespoons dijon-style mustard
1 tablespoon soy sauce
1 (12 ounce) jar peach preserves
2 (1 pound) pork tenderloins

- Preheat oven to 325°.

- In saucepan, combine mustard, soy sauce and peach preserves. Heat and stir until mixture mixes well. Place tenderloins in sprayed baking pan, spoon peach mixture over pork and sprinkle a little salt and black pepper over top.

- Cover and bake for 1 hour and remove from oven. Remove foil covering and return to oven for 25 minutes. Let stand at room temperature for about 15 minutes before slicing. Serves 8.

Savory Pork Chops

6 (½ inch) thick pork chops
1 tablespoon soy sauce
½ cup thick-and-chunky salsa
½ cup honey

- Preheat oven to 325°.

- In large skillet, brown pork chops in a little oil. Place browned chops in sprayed 9 x 13-inch baking pan.

- In small bowl, combine soy sauce, salsa, honey and ⅓ cup water. Pour mixture over pork chops. Cover with foil and bake for 50 minutes. Serve over hot, cooked rice. Serves 6.

Since God so loved us, we also ought to love one another. First John 4:11

Stuffing Over Pork Chops

1 (6 ounce) box savory herb stuffing mix
¼ cup (½ stick) butter, melted
6 center-cut pork chops
3 onions, halved horizontally

- Preheat oven to 350°.

- Prepare stuffing mix according to package directions with water called for and ¼ cup melted butter. Set aside.

- In sprayed skillet over medium-high heat, brown pork chops and place in sprayed 9 x 13-inch baking pan.

- Top each pork chop with 1 onion slice and stuffing over top of each onion. (If you have a large ice cream dipper, you can use that to place stuffing over onion and pork chop.)

- Cover and bake for 20 minutes. Remove cover and continue baking another 10 minutes. Serves 6.

Savory Sauce
Over Pork Tenderloin

2 (1 pound) pork tenderloins, cut in 1-inch cubes
1 (15 ounce) can pineapple chunks with liquid
1 (12 ounce) bottle chili sauce
1 teaspoon ground ginger

- Season pork tenderloin cubes with a little salt and pepper and place in large, sprayed skillet. Stir in pineapple chunks, chili sauce and ginger and mix well.

- Stir over high heat until mixture is thoroughly hot. Reduce heat to low, cover skillet and simmer 1½ hours. Serve over hot, cooked rice. Serves 6.

Tortellini-Ham Supper

2 (9 ounce) packages fresh tortellini
1 (10 ounce) package frozen green peas, thawed
1 (16 ounce) jar alfredo sauce
2 - 3 cups cubed ham

- Cook tortellini according to package directions. Add green peas about 5 minutes before tortellini is done. Drain.

- In saucepan, heat alfredo sauce and ham until thoroughly hot. Toss with tortellini and peas. Serves 8 to 10.

Sweet Potato Ham

1 (16 ounce/1½ inch) fully cooked ham slice
1 (18 ounce) can sweet potatoes, drained
½ cup packed brown sugar
⅓ cup chopped pecans

- Preheat oven to 350°.

- Slit outer edge of fat on ham slice at 1-inch intervals to prevent curling, but do not cut into ham. Place on 10-inch ovenproof, glass pie plate and broil with top 5 inches from heat for 5 minutes.

- In bowl, mash sweet potatoes with fork just once (not totally mashed). Add brown sugar, a little salt and chopped pecans and mix well.

- Spoon mixture over ham slice and bake for about 15 minutes. Serve right from pie plate. Serves 6.

He who searches after evil, it will come to him. Proverbs 11:27

Ravioli and Tomatoes

1 (9 ounce) package sausage-filled ravioli
1 (15 ounce) can Italian-stewed tomatoes
2 (4 ounce) cans sliced mushrooms
1 (5 ounce) package grated parmesan cheese

- Cook ravioli according to package directions and drain well. Stir in stewed tomatoes and mushrooms and bring to a boil. Reduce heat to low and simmer for about 5 minutes.
- Transfer to serving dish and sprinkle cheese on each serving. Serves 4 to 6.

Pork Chop Supper

1 (18 ounce) package smoked pork chops (5 - 6 chops)
1 (12 ounce) jar pork gravy
¼ cup milk
1 (12 ounce) package very small new (red) potatoes with peel

- In large skillet with a little oil, brown pork chops. Pour gravy and milk into skillet and stir mixture around chops until it mixes well. Add washed potatoes with peel around chops and gravy. Place lid on skillet and simmer on medium heat for about 15 minutes or until potatoes are tender. Serves 6.

What good is it for a man to gain the whole world, and yet lose or forfeit his very self? Luke 9:25

4 Ingredient Main Dishes: Pork

Ham and Veggies

2 (16 ounce) packages mixed vegetables
2 (10 ounce) cans cream of celery soup
2 cups cubed, cooked ham
½ teaspoon dried basil

- Cook vegetables according to package directions.
- Add soup, ham and basil.
- Cook until thoroughly hot and serve immediately. Serves 6.

Orange Pork Chops

6 - 8 medium-thick pork chops
¼ cup (½ stick) butter
2¼ cups orange juice
2 tablespoons orange marmalade

- Brown both sides of pork chops in butter in hot skillet and add a little salt and pepper.
- Pour orange juice over chops. Cover and simmer until done, about 1 hour. (Time will vary with thickness of pork chops.) Add more orange juice if necessary.
- During last few minutes of cooking, add 2 tablespoons orange marmalade. Serves 6.

TIP: This makes a delicious gravy to serve over rice.

I will praise the Lord according to his righteousness; and will sing to the name of the Lord most high. Psalm 7:17

Alfredo Salmon and Noodles

1 (12 ounce) package medium egg noodles
1 (16 ounce) package frozen broccoli florets, thawed
1 cup prepared alfredo sauce
1 (15 ounce) can salmon, drained, boned, flaked

- In large saucepan, cook noodles according to package direc-
  tions and add broccoli during last 5 minutes of cooking.
  Drain.
- Stir in alfredo sauce and salmon and cook on low heat,
  stirring occasionally, until mixture heats thoroughly.
  Spoon into serving bowl. Serves 8.

Shrimp and Crab Casserole

1 (6 ounce) can shrimp, drained
1 (6 ounce) can crabmeat, flaked, drained
1 (10 ounce) can corn chowder
1½ cups seasoned breadcrumbs, divided

- Preheat oven to 350°.
- In bowl, combine shrimp, crabmeat and corn chowder;
  stir in ½ cup breadcrumbs. Spoon into sprayed 1½-
  quart baking dish. Sprinkle remaining crumbs over top
  of casserole. Bake, uncovered, for 15 minutes or until
  bubbly and breadcrumbs are light brown. Serves 4.

*He who loves a pure heart and whose speech is gracious will have a king
for his friend. Proverbs 22:!1*

Scalloped Cabbage

2 small cabbages, cut up
1 (10 ounce) can cream of celery soup
1 cup shredded cheddar cheese
⅓ cup crumbled saltine crackers

- Preheat oven to 350°.
- Cut whole cabbages into quarters to easily remove thick white core. Place cut up cabbage in saucepan with 2 cups water and 1 teaspoon salt. Cook 8 minutes and drain. Transfer cabbage to sprayed 2-quart baking dish.
- In saucepan on medium heat, combine celery soup, ½ cup water and cheddar cheese; whisk, stirring constantly, until mixture is heated and cheese begins to melt. Pour mixture over cabbage and sprinkle with crumbled crackers. Bake uncovered 30 minutes. Serves 4 to 6.

Chili-Baked Beans

2 (16 ounce) cans pork and beans
1 (15 ounce) can chili with beans
¼ cup molasses
1 teaspoon chili powder

- Pour visible liquid from can of pork and beans.
- In 2-quart baking dish, combine pork and beans, chili, molasses and chili powder. Heat until bubbly. Serves 6.

Thou hast faith, and I have works: Show me thy faith without thy works and I will show thee my faith by my works. James 2:18

Brown Sugar Carrots

¼ cup (½ stick) butter
¾ cup packed brown sugar
½ teaspoon cinnamon
1 (16 ounce) package peeled baby carrots

- In skillet, combine butter, brown sugar, cinnamon and ½ cup water; cook on medium heat until bubbly.
- Stir in carrots, cover and cook on medium heat until carrots glaze and are tender. Serves 6.

Cheesy Summer Squash

8 medium yellow squash
1 bell pepper, seeded, chopped
1 onion, chopped
1 (8 ounce) package shredded Velveeta® cheese

- Preheat oven to 350°.
- Combine squash, bell pepper and onion in large saucepan with just enough water to barely cover vegetables. Cook over medium-high heat until tender-crisp, about 10 minutes. Drain and keep squash in same saucepan.
- Gently fold in cheese and spoon into sprayed 2-quart baking dish. Cover and bake 15 minutes. Serves 8.

Do not judge, or you too will be judged. Matthew 7:1

4 Ingredient Vegetables

Creamed Asparagus

4 bunches fresh asparagus
2 teaspoons dried basil
4 (10 ounce) cans cream of asparagus soup
1½ cups prepared Italian breadcrumbs

- Preheat oven to 325°.
- Cut off tough ends of stalks and place in sprayed 7 x 11-inch baking dish. Sprinkle with basil and a little salt. Bake uncovered for 10 minutes.
- Place cream of asparagus soup in skillet with ⅓ cup water (or milk); heat just enough to mix with water. Spread over baked asparagus and sprinkle with Italian breadcrumbs. Bake for 30 minutes; serve from baking dish. Serves 8.

Oven Baked Asparagus

2 bunches fresh asparagus, trimmed
4 tablespoons extra-virgin olive oil
4 tablespoons balsamic vinegar
¾ cup fresh grated parmesan cheese

- Preheat oven to 400°.
- Arrange asparagus in single layer in sprayed baking dish and drizzle olive oil over asparagus. Bake uncovered about 10 minutes or until asparagus is tender.
- To serve, sprinkle with a little salt and pepper, vinegar and parmesan cheese. Serves 8.

Yet I am always with you; you hold me by my right hand. Psalm 73:23

Creamy Cauliflower

1 large head cauliflower, broken into large florets
1 red bell pepper, seeded, chopped
1 (10 ounce) can cream of celery soup
½ cup milk

- Place cauliflower florets and red bell pepper in saucepan with about ¾ cup water and a little salt. Cover and cook on high heat about 10 minutes or until cauliflower is tender. Drain and keep warm.

- In smaller saucepan combine soup and milk, heat and stir until they mix well. Spoon cauliflower and bell pepper into serving bowl and pour soup mixture over vegetables. Serve immediately. Serves 8.

Simply Sweet Carrots

1 (16 ounce) package baby carrots
1 (14 ounce) can chicken broth
½ cup apricot preserves
1 tablespoon soy sauce

- Place carrots and broth in saucepan and bring to a boil. Reduce heat to medium and cook for about 14 minutes or until carrots are tender-crisp and liquid reduces to about ¼ cup.

- Stir in apricot preserves and soy sauce; cook another 10 minutes. Stir constantly until mixture thickens and carrots glaze. Serves 6.

Your world is a lamp on my feet and a light for my path. Psalm 119:105

4 Ingredient Vegetables

Zucchini and Creamy Penne

6 - 8 medium zucchini, sliced
2 (16 ounce) packages penne pasta
2 (8 ounce) cartons whipping cream
12 ounces crumbled goat cheese

- In saucepan, cook zucchini in a little salted water, drain and add 1 tablespoon olive oil. Cook penne according to package directions. Drain and add another tablespoon olive oil.

- While zucchini and pasta are still hot, combine ingredients, stir in whipping cream and goat cheese and toss. Serve hot. Serves 8.

Cheesy Baked Onions

4 yellow onions, peeled, sliced
½ cup (1 stick) butter
25 round, cheesy round crackers, crushed
⅓ cup grated parmesan cheese

- Preheat oven to 325°.
- Saute onions in butter until transparent.
- Spread half onions in sprayed 2-quart baking dish. Top with half crackers and half cheese. Repeat layers.
- Bake uncovered for 30 minutes.

Look at the birds of the air; they do not sow or reap or store away in barns, and yet your heavenly Father feeds them. Are you not much more valuable than they? Matthew 6:26

Maple-Pecan Sweet Potatoes

½ cup chopped, toasted pecans
1 (29 ounce) can sweet potatoes, drained
¼ cup (½ stick) butter, melted
½ cup pure maple syrup

- Preheat oven to 350°.
- Toast pecans in oven about 10 minutes. In bowl, mash sweet potatoes with fork, but leave some small chunks.
- Add melted butter and maple syrup; mix well. Transfer to sprayed 7 x 11-inch baking dish.
- Sprinkle pecans over sweet potato mixture and bake uncovered for 25 minutes. Serves 6 to 8.

Favorite Fettuccine

1 (16 ounce) package fettuccine
2 tablespoons butter
¾ cup grated fresh parmesan cheese
1¼ cups whipping cream

- Cook fettuccine according to package directions.
- In large saucepan over medium heat, melt butter and stir in parmesan cheese, cream and a little black pepper.
- Cook 1 minute and stir constantly. Reduce heat, pour in fettuccine and toss gently to coat. Serves 6.

Lead me, O Lord in your righteousness...make straight your way before me. Psalm 5:8

Tasty Rice Bake

1½ cups rice
½ cup (1 stick) butter, melted
1 (10 ounce) can French onion soup
1 (8 ounce) can sliced water chestnuts, drained

- Preheat oven to 350°.
- Combine rice, butter, soup, water chestnuts and 1¼ cups water.
- Pour into sprayed 2-quart baking dish. Bake covered for 1 hour. Serves 6.

Wonderful Alfredo Fettuccine

2 (16 ounce) packages uncooked fettuccine
¼ cup (½ stick) butter
1½ cups grated fresh parmesan cheese
2½ cups whipping cream

- Cook fettuccine according to package directions.
- In large saucepan over medium heat, melt butter and stir in parmesan cheese, cream and a little salt. Cook 2 minutes and stir constantly. Reduce heat and stir into fettuccine and toss gently to coat. Serves 10 to 12.

You have filled my heart with a greater joy. Psalm 4:7

Cheesy New Potatoes

½ cup (1 stick) butter, melted
¼ cup grated parmesan cheese
½ teaspoon white pepper
12 small-medium red (new) potatoes

- Preheat oven to 375°.
- Melt butter in 9 x 13-inch baking dish and sprinkle cheese, white pepper and a little salt over butter. Cut potatoes in half and place, cut side down in baking dish.
- Bake uncovered for 45 minutes or until potatoes are tender. Serves 6 to 8.

Instant Beans and Rice

1 (8.8 ounce) package brown rice
1 (15 ounce) can pinto beans with liquid
½ cup hot thick-and-chunky salsa
1 teaspoon cumin

- Preheat oven to 325°.
- Microwave rice in package for 90 seconds. Transfer to saucepan and add beans, salsa, cumin and a little salt.
- Spoon into a sprayed 7 x 11-inch baking dish. Cover and bake for 25 minutes.

And forgive our debts, as we forgive our debtors. Matthew 6:12

Carnival Couscous

1 (6 ounce) box herbed-chicken couscous
¼ cup (½ stick) butter
1 red bell pepper, diced
1 yellow squash, diced
¾ cup fresh broccoli florets, finely chopped

- Cook couscous according to package directions, but leave out butter.
- With butter in saucepan, saute bell pepper, squash and broccoli and cook about 10 minutes or until vegetables are almost tender.
- Combine couscous and vegetables. Serve hot. Serves 8.

Cinnamon Baked Apples

8 Granny Smith apples
1 cup mixed nuts
1¼ cups packed light brown sugar
1½ teaspoons cinnamon

- Preheat oven to 350°.
- Core apples without cutting through to bottom. Use a potato peeler to peel a 1-inch strip around top of apple.
- Combine nuts, sugar and cinnamon and stuff cavities with mixture and place apples in sprayed 2-quart baking dish. Drizzle apple with 2 tablespoons water and bake about 45 minutes or until apples are tender when pierced with a knife.
- Serve warm or at room temperature. Serves 6 to 8.

Cheddar-Tomato Bread

3 cups baking mix
1 cup finely shredded cheddar cheese
2 eggs
1 (15 ounce) can diced tomatoes

• Preheat oven to 350°.

• Spray 2 (9-inch) loaf pans. In bowl, combine baking mix, cheese and a little salt. Make a well in the middle and stir in eggs, ⅓ cup water and tomatoes. Stir until dry ingredients are very moist. Divide evenly between 2 loaf pans.

• Bake for 45 minutes or until toothpick inserted in center comes out clean. Cool slightly before turning out on rack. Serve warm. Serves 10 to 12.

 # Lariat Bread Knots

¼ cup (½ stick) butter
½ teaspoon chili powder
½ teaspoon ground cumin
1 (11 ounce) can refrigerated breadstick dough

• Preheat oven to 350°.

• In saucepan, melt butter and stir in chili powder and ground cumin.

• Unroll breadsticks and separate each portion. Loosely tie each portion into a knot and place on sprayed baking sheet about 1-inch apart.

• With kitchen brush, spread butter mixture evenly over bread knots. Bake for 15 minutes or until breadsticks are light brown. Serves 6.

4 Ingredient Breads

French Cheese Loaf

1 (16 ounce) loaf unsliced French bread
½ cup (1 stick) butter, softened
1 teaspoon minced garlic
1 (4 ounce) package crumbled blue cheese

- Preheat oven to 375°.
- Slice bread at 1-inch intervals, but not through bottom of loaf.
- In bowl, combine softened butter, garlic and blue cheese and spread evenly on both sides of each bread slice. Wrap loaf in foil and place on large baking pan.
- Bake for 15 minutes or until bread is thoroughly hot. Serves 8.

Garlic Rounds

2 teaspoons minced garlic
3 teaspoons dried parsley flakes
2 tablespoons olive oil
1 (13 ounce) package refrigerated pizza crust

- Preheat oven to 400°.
- In small bowl, combine garlic, parsley flakes and olive oil.
- On flat surface, unroll pizza dough, brush with garlic-oil mixture and roll dough again.
- Use serrated knife to cut into 1-inch pieces and place each piece in sprayed muffin pan. Brush any remaining garlic mixture over top of rounds.
- Bake for 15 minutes or until golden brown. Serves 6.

Give us today our daily bread. Matthew 6:11

4 Ingredient Breads

Jack's Breadsticks

1 (11 ounce) can refrigerated breadstick dough
⅓ cup finely shredded Monterey Jack cheese with jalapenos
½ teaspoon ground cumin
½ teaspoon garlic powder

- Preheat oven to 375°.
- Place dough on flat surface and cut along perforations to form 12 breadsticks. Combine cheese, cumin and garlic powder, sprinkle over breadsticks and press into dough. Twist each breadstick and place on sprayed baking sheet.
- Bake for 14 minutes or until light brown. Serves 6.

Cheese Bread

1 (16 ounce) package shredded, sharp cheddar cheese
1 cup mayonnaise
1 (1 ounce) packet ranch-style dressing mix
10 (1 inch) slices French bread

- Preheat oven to 400°.
- Combine cheese, mayonnaise and dressing mix.
- Spread on bread slices and heat for 10 to 15 minutes or until toast begins to brown. Serves 6.

I served the Lord with great humility and tears. Acts 20:19

Carrot-Apple Salad

1 (16 ounce) package shredded carrots
2 green apples with peel, chopped
1 tablespoon mayonnaise
1 tablespoon lemon juice

- In bowl, combine shredded carrots and apples. Add mayonnaise and lemon juice and toss. Refrigerate. Serves 8.

Festive Cranberry Salad

1 (6 ounce) package raspberry gelatin
1 (20 ounce) can crushed pineapple
1 (16 ounce) can whole cranberries
⅔ cup chopped walnuts

- Place gelatin in bowl, pour in 1½ cups boiling water and mix well. Stir in pineapple, cranberries and walnuts.
- Transfer to glass 7 x 11-inch baking dish. Chill several hours. Cut into squares to serve. Serves 8.

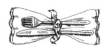

Encourage one another daily. Hebrews 3:13

Festive Green and Yellow Veggie Salad

4 - 5 cups small broccoli florets
4 small yellow squash, seeded, cubed
2 red bell peppers, seeded, chopped
1 (8 ounce) bottle zesty Italian salad dressing

- In large salad bowl with lid combine broccoli, squash and bell pepper; mix well.
- Spoon dressing over salad and toss. Cover and refrigerate several hours before serving. Serves 8.

Special Macaroni Salad

2 (16 ounce) cartons prepared macaroni salad
2 (8 ounce) cans whole kernel corn, drained
4 small zucchini, diced
1⅓ cups chunky salsa

- In salad bowl with lid, combine macaroni salad, corn, zucchini and salsa and mix well. Cover and refrigerate until ready to serve. Serves 8.

He who pursues righteousness and love finds life, prosperity and honor.
Proverbs 21:21

4 Ingredient Salads

Cherry Crush

1 (6 ounce) box cherry gelatin
1 (8 ounce) package cream cheese, softened
1 (20 ounce) can cherry pie filling
1 (15 ounce) can crushed pineapple with juice

- Dissolve gelatin with 1¼ cups boiling water.
- With electric mixer beat in cream cheese very slowly at first. Fold in pie filling and crushed pineapple.
- Pour into 9 x 13-inch baking dish. Refrigerate. Serves 8.

Quick Potato Salad

3 - 4 baking potatoes
½ cup diced dill or sweet pickles
3 eggs, hard-boiled, chopped
¾ - 1 cup mayonnaise

- Cook potatoes (potatoes can be cooked the night before using) in microwave and when cooled, peel and cut into 1-inch cubes. Place in large bowl. Add pickles (pickle relish can be used), chopped eggs, an ample amount of salt and pepper.
- Stir in ¾ cup mayonnaise and more if potato salad is too dry. Refrigerate. If making salad to be eaten immediately, it can be served at room temperature. Serves 4.

I love the Lord...because he turned his ear to me, I will call on him as long as I live. Psalm 116:1,2

Orange Glow

1 (6 ounce) package orange gelatin
1 cup finely grated carrots
1 (15 ounce) can crushed pineapple with juice
¾ cup chopped pecans

- Combine gelatin in 1 cup boiling water and mix well.
- Add carrots, pineapple and pecans.
- Pour into 7 x 11-inch glass dish. Refrigerate until it congeals. Serves 6.

Noodle-Turkey Salad

1 (3 ounce) package oriental-flavor ramen noodle soup mix
1 (16 ounce) package finely shredded coleslaw mix
¾ pound deli smoked turkey, cut into strips
½ cup prepared vinaigrette salad dressing

- Coarsely crush noodles and place in bowl with a lid. Add coleslaw mix and turkey strips.
- In small bowl, combine vinaigrette salad dressing and seasoning packet from noodle mix. Pour over noodle-turkey mixture and toss to coat mixture well.
- Refrigerate. Serves 4 to 6.

But Peter said unto him, "Thy money perish with thee, because thou hast thought that the gift of God may be purchased with money."
Acts 8:20

4 Ingredient Salads

Mandarin Fluff

2 (11 ounce) cans mandarin oranges, well drained
1 cup miniature marshmallows
1 (8 ounce) carton whipped topping
½ cup chopped pecans

- Place oranges in bowl and stir in marshmallows. (Make sure marshmallows are not stuck together.)
- Fold in whipped topping and pecans and chill. Spoon into small crystal bowl, cover and refrigerate. Serves 4 to 6.

Cherry-Cranberry Salad

1 (6 ounce) package cherry gelatin
1 (20 ounce) can cherry pie filling
1 (16 ounce) can whole cranberry sauce

- In mixing bowl, combine cherry gelatin and 1 cup boiling water and mix until gelatin dissolves.
- Mix pie filling and cranberry sauce into gelatin.
- Pour into 9 x 13-inch dish and refrigerate. Serves 6.

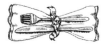

Search me, O God, and know my heart; try me, and know my thoughts.
Psalm 139:23

Cucumber-Onion Salad

4 - 6 seedless cucumbers, peeled, sliced
4 onions, sliced
2 tablespoons white vinegar
1 cup sour cream

- In mixing bowl, sprinkle 1 teaspoon salt over cucumbers and let stand 20 minutes; drain. Add onions and vinegar and toss. Refrigerate.
- When ready to serve, stir in sour cream. Serves 8.

Cheesy Vegetable Salad

4 seedless cucumbers, coarsely chopped
2 sweet red bell peppers, julienned
2 sweet (Vidalia) onions, coarsely chopped
2 cups crumbled feta cheese

- In salad bowl, combine cucumbers, bell pepper, onion and feta cheese and toss with 1 cup vinaigrette salad dressing. Add more dressing if needed Serves 8.

We know that all things work together for good to those who love God. Romans 8:28

Dreamy-Creamy Dessert

28 chocolate cream-filled chocolate cookies, divided
2½ cups milk
3 (3.4 ounce) packages instant pistachio pudding
1 (8 ounce) carton whipped topping

- Crush cookies and reserve ⅔ cup for topping. Place remaining crushed cookies in 9 x 13-inch glass dish.
- In mixing bowl, combine milk and pistachio pudding; stir well, about 2 minutes, until pudding mixes well. Pour over crushed cookies and spread out with back of large spoon.
- Spread whipped topping over pudding and sprinkle with remaining crushed cookies. Refrigerate overnight before serving. Cut into squares to serve. Serves 8 to 10.

Peanut Butter Drops

1 cup sugar
¾ cup light corn syrup
1 (16 ounce) jar crunchy peanut butter
4½ cups chow mein noodles

- In saucepan over medium heat, bring sugar and corn syrup to a boil; stir in peanut butter.
- Remove from heat and stir in chow mein noodles. Drop by tablespoonfuls onto wax paper and allow to cool completely. Serves 12.

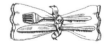

4 Ingredient Desserts

Fruit Medley

2 cups red grapes, halved, chilled
3 cups cubed honeydew melon, chilled
2 (15 ounce) cans pineapple tidbits, drained, chilled
1 cup peach preserves

- In large salad bowl, combine grapes, melon and pineapple. In saucepan, heat preserves about 5 minutes or just until they mix well with fruit.

- Stir in peach preserves and gently toss to coat. Chill before serving. Serves 8.

Walnut Squares

1⅔ cups graham cracker crumbs
1½ cups coarsely chopped walnuts
1 (14 ounce) can sweetened condensed milk
⅓ cup flaked coconut

- Preheat oven to 350°.

- Place graham cracker crumbs and walnuts in bowl and slowly add sweetened condensed milk, coconut and pinch of salt. Mixture will be very thick.

- Spoon into sprayed 9-inch baking pan. Pack mixture down with back of large spoon. Bake for 30 minutes and cut into squares when cool. Serves 10.

So the son of man must be lifted up that everyone who believes in him may have eternal life. John 3:14,15

4 Ingredient Desserts

Quick Summer Cake

1 (16 ounce) frozen loaf pound cake
1 (8 ounce) carton whipping cream
1 (20 ounce) can coconut pie filling
2 kiwifruit, peeled, halved, sliced

- Split cake into 3 horizontal layers and place bottom layer on serving platter.
- With mixer, beat whipping cream until thick and fold in coconut pie filling. Mix until they blend well. Spread one-third mixture over bottom cake layer.
- Place second layer on top and spread half remaining cream mixture on top. Top with third layer and spread remaining cream mixture on top.
- Garnish with slices of kiwifruit over top of cake. Refrigerate. Serves 8 to 10.

Extreme Pound Cake

1 (9 inch) round bakery pound cake
1 (20 ounce) can crushed pineapple with juice
1 (4 serving) instant vanilla pudding or pie filling
1 (8 ounce) carton whipped topping, divided

- Cut pound cake horizontally into 3 layers and place bottom layer on cake plate.
- In bowl, gently combine and mix crushed pineapple and pudding. When they mix well, fold in half whipped topping.
- Spread one-third pineapple mixture over top of bottom layer (not on sides). Place second cake layer on top and spread half remaining pineapple mixture.
- Top with third cake layer and remaining pineapple mixture. Top with remaining whipped topping.
- Refrigerate. Serves 8 to 10.

Crowd Pleasers

Fabulous recipes for groups of 20... Easy on planners and cooks – Expecting 40? Make 2, 60? Make 3...It's that easy!

Vegetables and Side Dishes......... 212

Chicken... 221

Beef.. 229

Pork 231

Seafood 235

Desserts... 237

 Corn Success

2 (15 ounce) cans cream-style corn
2 (15 ounce) cans whole kernel corn, drained
1 bell pepper, seeded, chopped
1 onion, chopped
1 (10 ounce) can tomatoes and green chilies
¼ cup (½ stick) butter, melted
3 eggs, beaten
1 teaspoon sugar
1 teaspoon seasoned salt
1 cup buttery cracker crumbs
1 (8 ounce) package shredded Mexican 4-cheese blend

- Preheat oven to 350°.
- Mix cans of corn, bell pepper, onion, tomatoes and green chilies, butter, eggs, sugar, salt and cracker crumbs in large mixing bowl.
- Pour into sprayed 10 x 15-inch baking dish.
- Bake uncovered for 45 minutes. Remove from oven, sprinkle cheese over casserole and return to oven for 5 minutes. Serves 20.

How great is the love the Father has lavished on us, that we should be called children of God! First John 3:1

Corn That Pleases

You will probably find this popular corn casserole or a very similar version at lots of church suppers. And the dish will always be empty by the end of the evening.

3 (15 ounce) cans whole kernel corn
2 (15 ounce) cans cream-style corn
½ cup (1 stick) butter, melted
3 eggs, beaten
1 (16 ounce) carton sour cream
1 (8 ounce) package jalapeno cornbread mix
1 cup shredded cheddar cheese

- Preheat oven to 350°.
- Mix all ingredients, except cheese in large bowl. Pour into sprayed 10 x 15-inch baking dish.
- Bake uncovered for 40 to 45 minutes. Uncover and sprinkle cheese on top of casserole. Return to oven for 5 minutes. Serves 20.

Casting all your care upon him: for he careth for you. First Peter 5:7

Carrots Bring Sunshine

This is absolutely the prettiest casserole you will place on your table! And not only pretty, but it is also delicious and elegant. You'll never want a simple, buttered carrot again!

4 cups finely shredded carrots
3 cups cooked instant rice
3 eggs, beaten
1 (12 ounce) package cubed Velveeta® cheese
2 (15 ounce) can cream-style corn
1 (8 ounce) carton whipping cream
¼ cup (½ stick) butter, melted
3 tablespoons dried minced onion
1½ teaspoons seasoned salt
½ teaspoon white pepper

- Preheat oven to 350°.
- In large bowl, combine all ingredients. Spoon into sprayed 1 (10 x 15-inch) or 2 (2-quart) baking dishes.
- Bake uncovered for 45 minutes or until set. Serves 20.

TIP: If you don't have white pepper and do not mind the black specks, black pepper will be fine to use.

Great are the works of the Lord; they are pondered by all who delight in them.
Psalm 111:2

Creamy Spinach To Love

2 (16 ounce) packages frozen chopped spinach
2 (8 ounce) packages cream cheese and chives, softened
1 (8 ounce) package shredded cheddar cheese
1 (10 ounce) can cream of celery soup
1 cup milk
2 eggs, beaten
2 cups cheese cracker crumbs

- Preheat oven to 350°.
- Cook spinach in saucepan according to package direc-tions and drain well.
- Add cream cheese and cheddar cheese to hot spinach, stir until cheese melts and mixes well.
- Stir in soup, milk and eggs and mix well.
- Pour into sprayed 2 (2-quart) baking dishes or 1 (10 x 15-inch) baking dish. Top with cheese cracker crumbs.
- Bake small casserole uncovered for 35 minutes and larger casserole for 45 minutes. Serves 20.

Wise men store up knowledge, but with the foolish, ruin is at hand.
Proverbs 10:14

Yellow Squash Deluxe

8 - 9 cups sliced yellow squash
1 large onion, chopped
1 carrot, finely grated
1 (8 ounce) package cream cheese, softened, cubed
1 (4 ounce) jar chopped pimento, drained
1 (8 ounce) carton sour cream
1 (15 ounce) carton small curd cottage cheese, drained
1 (8 ounce) package shredded Monterey Jack cheese
½ cup (1 stick) butter, melted, divided
1 (6 ounce) package chicken-flavor stuffing mix, divided

- Preheat oven to 350°.
- Cook squash, onion and grated carrot in a little salted water in large saucepan until tender-crisp. Drain.
- While mixture is still hot, fold in cream cheese and stir until it melts.
- Add pimento, sour cream, cottage cheese, Monterey Jack cheese and about 4 tablespoons (½ stick) melted butter and mix well.
- Stir in half stuffing mix and all of seasoning package included with mix; fold into squash mixture. Spoon into lightly sprayed 10 x 15-inch baking dish.
- Sprinkle remaining stuffing over top and drizzle remaining melted butter over top.
- Bake uncovered for 45 minutes. Serves 20.

We love because he first loved us. First John 4:19

Cheesy Broccoli-Rice Bake

So easy and so good! It gives us a vegetable and rice all in one dish.

2½ cups instant rice
1 cup onion, chopped
1 large red bell pepper, seeded, chopped
1 cup chopped celery
½ cup (1 stick) butter
1 (12 ounce) package shredded Mexican Velveeta® cheese
2 (10 ounce) cans cream of chicken soup
¾ cup whole milk
1 (16 ounce) package frozen chopped broccoli, thawed, drained

- Preheat oven to 350°.
- Cook rice according to package directions in large saucepan.
- Saute onions, bell pepper and celery in butter. Add onion-celery mixture to rice. Fold in cheese, chicken soup and milk and mix well.
- Heat on low until cheese and soup blend well. Fold in broccoli.
- Pour into sprayed 10 x 15-inch baking dish, cover and bake for 45 minutes. Serves 20.

O Lord, our Lord, how majestic is your name in all the earth! Psalm 8:1

Potato Supreme

This is no time to count calories!

7 - 8 large baking potatoes, cooked in microwave
1 cup half-and-half cream
½ cup (1 stick) butter, sliced
1 (12 ounce) package shredded cheddar cheese
1 (16 ounce) carton sour cream
2 teaspoons seasoned salt
1 teaspoon white pepper
1 bunch green onions with tops, sliced

- Preheat oven to 350°.
- Cool potatoes; peel and grate.
- Combine cream, butter, cheese, sour cream, seasoned salt and white pepper in double boiler; cook and stir just until butter and cheese melt.
- Add cheese mixture to grated potatoes and place in sprayed 10 x 15-inch baking dish.
- Cover and bake for 35 to 40 minutes. To serve, top with sliced green onions. Serves 20.

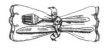

Stand firm in the Lord. Philippians 4:1

Awesome Sweet Potatoes

This is a beautiful Thanksgiving dish and perfect for Christmas dinner too.
Even people who are "luke warm" about sweet potatoes like this casserole.

2 (29 ounce) cans sweet potatoes, drained
⅔ cup evaporated milk
1½ cups sugar
1 cup packed brown sugar
3 eggs, beaten
½ cup (1 stick) butter, melted
1 teaspoon vanilla

- Preheat oven to 350°.
- Place sweet potatoes in mixing bowl and mash slightly with fork.
- Add evaporated milk, both sugars, eggs, butter and vanilla; mix well. Pour into sprayed 2 (2-quart) baking dishes or 1 (10 x 15-inch) baking dish.

Topping:
2 cups packed light brown sugar
½ cup (1 stick) butter, melted
1 cup flour
1½ cups chopped pecans

- For topping, combine brown sugar, butter and flour and mix well. Stir in chopped pecans and sprinkle topping over casserole. Bake uncovered for 35 to 45 minutes or until crusty on top. Serves 20.

And whatsoever ye do in word or deed, do all in the name of the Lord Jesus.
Colossians 3:17

Side Dishes for 20+

Cranberries Supreme

What a great dish for the holidays!

3 (20 ounce) cans pie apples*
2 (16 ounce) can whole cranberries
2 cups sugar
½ cup packed brown sugar

- Preheat oven to 325°.
- Combine pie apples, cranberries and both sugars in bowl and mix well. Spoon into sprayed 10 x 15-inch baking dish.

Topping:
⅓ cup (¾ stick) butter
2½ cups crushed corn flakes
1 cup sugar
½ teaspoon ground cinnamon
1½ cups chopped pecans

- Melt butter in saucepan and mix in corn flakes, sugar, cinnamon and pecans.
- Sprinkle over apples and cranberries.
- Bake uncovered for 1 hour. This can be served hot or at room temperature. Serves 20.

TIP: Look for pie apples, not apple pie filling. They are near the pie fillings.

Lazy hands make a man poor, but diligent hands bring wealth. Proverbs 10:4

Side Dishes for 20+

Creamy, Cheesy Spaghetti Chicken

1 bunch fresh green onions, with tops, chopped
1 cup chopped celery
1 yellow and 1 red bell pepper, seeded, chopped
¼ cup (½ stick) butter
2 teaspoons Italian seasoning
1 (12 ounce) package thin spaghetti, cooked, drained
4 cups cooked, chopped chicken or turkey
1 (8 ounce) carton sour cream
1 (16 ounce) jar creamy alfredo sauce
1 (10 ounce) box frozen green peas, thawed
1 (16 ounce) package shredded mozzarella cheese, divided

- Preheat oven to 350°.
- Saute onions, celery and bell peppers in large skillet with butter.
- In large bowl combine onion-pepper mixture, seasoning, a little salt and pepper, spaghetti, chicken, sour cream and alfredo sauce; mix well.
- Fold in peas and half the mozzarella cheese and spoon into sprayed 10 x 15-inch deep baking dish. Cover and bake for 50 minutes.
- Remove from oven and sprinkle remaining cheese over casserole. Return to oven for about 5 minutes. Serves 20.

Do not neglect your gift. First Timothy 4:14

A Deal of a Chicken Bake

This is such a good basic "meat and potatoes" recipe; everyone loves it.

¼ cup (½ stick) butter
1 (16 ounce) package frozen peppers and onions
3 ribs celery, chopped
1 (16 ounce) carton sour cream
1 (7 ounce) can chopped green chilies, drained
1 teaspoon seasoned salt
1½ teaspoons white pepper
1 (14 ounce) can chicken broth
4 - 5 cups cooked, cubed chicken
1 (16 ounce) package shredded cheddar cheese, divided
1 (2 pound) package frozen hash brown potatoes, thawed

- Preheat oven to 350°.
- In saucepan, melt butter and saute peppers and onions and celery.
- In large bowl, combine sour cream, green chilies and seasonings. Stir in pepper-onion mixture, chicken broth, chicken and half the cheese.
- Fold in hash brown potatoes and spoon into sprayed 10 x 15-inch baking dish.
- Bake uncovered for 45 minutes or until casserole bubbles.
- Remove from oven and sprinkle remaining cheese over top of casserole. Return to oven for about 5 minutes. Serves 20.

It is more blessed to give than to receive. Acts 20:35

Cheesy Chicken Noodles

1 large onion, chopped
1 green and 1 red bell pepper, seeded, chopped
½ cup (1 stick) butter
1 (10 ounce) can cream of chicken soup
1 (14 ounce) can chicken broth
1 (4 ounce) can sliced mushrooms, drained
½ teaspoon dried basil
1 teaspoon seasoned salt
1 teaspoon garlic powder
1 (12 ounce) package egg noodles, cooked, drained
4 - 5 cups cooked, cubed chicken breasts
1 (15 ounce) carton ricotta cheese
1 (16 ounce) package shredded cheddar cheese
1½ cups seasoned breadcrumbs

- Preheat oven to 350°.
- In skillet, saute onion and bell peppers in butter. Remove from heat and stir in soup, chicken broth, mushrooms, basil, seasoned salt and garlic powder.
- In large bowl combine noodles, chicken, cheeses and soup-mushroom mixture. Mix well and spoon into sprayed 10 x 15-inch baking dish.
- Sprinkle breadcrumbs over casserole. Cover and bake for 50 to 55 minutes. Serves 20.

And we urge you ... be patient with everyone. First Thessalonians 5:14

Chicken for 20+

Fiesta Time for Chicken

This is another dish that is great for leftover turkey.

1 (16 ounce) package tortilla chips
4 cups cooked, chopped chicken breasts
1 large onion, chopped
1 green and 1 red bell pepper, seeded, chopped
1 (12 ounce) package shredded Mexican 4-cheese blend
1 teaspoon chili powder
1 teaspoon ground cumin
2 (10 ounce) cans cream of chicken soup
1 (15 ounce) can Mexican stewed tomatoes

- Preheat oven to 325°.
- Pour about two-thirds of tortilla chips into sprayed 10 x 15-inch baking dish and crush slightly with palm of your hand.
- In large bowl, combine chicken, onion, bell peppers, cheese, chili powder, 1 teaspoon pepper, cumin, soup and tomatoes and mix well. Spoon mixture over crushed tortilla chips.
- Crush remaining tortilla chips in plastic bag and spread over casserole.
- Bake uncovered for 45 to 50 minutes or until chips are light brown. Serves 20.

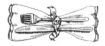

Search me O God, and know my heart: try me and know my thoughts.
Psalm 139:23

Veggie Cheesy Chicken

¾ cup (1½ sticks) butter, divided
¼ cup flour
1 (1 pint) carton half-and-half cream
1 (10 ounce) can chicken broth
2 (10 ounce) cans cream of chicken soup
1 (16 ounce) package frozen broccoli spears, thawed
1 (10 ounce) package frozen cauliflower, thawed
2 red bell peppers, seeded, thinly sliced
1 cup chopped celery
2 cups cooked brown rice
4 cups cooked, cubed chicken or turkey
1 (12 ounce) package shredded cheddar cheese
2 cups soft breadcrumbs

- Preheat oven to 350°.
- In saucepan, melt ½ cup (1 stick) butter in saucepan, add flour and stir until mixture is smooth.
- Slowly stir in cream and chicken broth. Cook and stir constantly until mixture is thick. Stir in soup until mixture blends well; set aside.
- Place broccoli, cauliflower, bell pepper and celery into sprayed 10 x 15-inch baking dish.
- Cover with rice, half the cream sauce and top with chicken. Stir shredded cheese into remaining sauce and pour over chicken.
- Melt remaining ¼ cup butter. Combine breadcrumbs and melted butter. Sprinkle over casserole.
- Bake uncovered for about 45 to 50 minutes or until casserole is thoroughly hot. Serves 20.

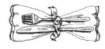

Walnuts Make the Chicken

Walnuts give this dish a special touch.
This casserole will get rave reviews.

2 (6 ounce) boxes long grain and wild rice
2 red bell peppers, seeded, chopped
2 cups chopped celery
1 large onion, chopped
2 cups coarsely chopped walnuts
½ cup (1 stick) butter
2 cups mayonnaise
1 (1 pint) carton sour cream
2 tablespoons lemon juice
2 teaspoons seasoned salt
4 cups cooked, cubed chicken
2 cups crushed potato chips

- Preheat oven to 325°.
- Cook rice according to package directions.
- In skillet, lightly saute bell peppers, celery, onion and walnuts in butter. Stir in mayonnaise, sour cream, lemon juice, seasoned salt and chicken; mix well.
- Fold in cooked rice and transfer to sprayed 10 x 15-inch baking dish.
- Sprinkle potato chips over top of casserole.
- Bake uncovered for 35 to 40 minutes or until potato chips are light brown. Serves 20.

There is surely a future hope for you, and your hope will not be cut off.
Proverbs 23:18

Dinner With the Italian Touch

Baked Italian dishes are famous for their rich, flavorful sauces.
This recipe is creamy, cheesy and delicious.

2 pounds ground round beef
1 onion, chopped
1 sweet red bell pepper, chopped
2 teaspoons minced garlic
1 (26 ounce) jar chunky spaghetti sauce
2 (8 ounce) jars sliced mushrooms, drained
1 teaspoon ground oregano
2 teaspoons Italian seasoning
1 (12 ounce) package medium egg noodles
1 (12 ounce) package ricotta cheese
1 (1 pint) carton sour cream
1 (5 ounce) package grated Parmesan cheese
1 (16 ounce) package shredded mozzarella cheese, divided

- Preheat oven to 325°.
- In very large skillet, brown beef, onion, bell pepper and garlic; drain well. Add spaghetti sauce, mushrooms, oregano, Italian seasoning and dash of salt and pepper. Heat to a boil, reduce heat and simmer about 15 minutes.
- Cook noodles according to package directions and drain.
- In large bowl, combine ricotta cheese, sour cream, Parmesan cheese and half mozzarella cheese.
- In sprayed 10 x 15-inch baking dish, layer half noodles, half beef mixture and half cheese mixture. Repeat layers.
- Cover and bake for 40 minutes. Remove covering and sprinkle with remaining mozzarella cheese. Bake another 5 to 10 minutes. Serves 20.

A Touch of Mexico

3 pounds lean ground beef
1 teaspoon seasoned salt
1 large onion, chopped
2 red bell peppers, seeded, chopped
1 green bell pepper, seeded, chopped
3 cups zucchini, chopped
1 (1 ounce) packet taco seasoning
¼ cup (½ stick) butter
2 cups instant rice
1 (16 ounce) jar chunky salsa
1 (12 ounce) package shredded Mexican Velveeta® cheese
2½ cups lightly crushed tortilla chips

- Preheat oven to 350°.

- Brown ground beef in large skillet, drain and add seasoned salt. Add onion, bell peppers, zucchini, taco seasoning and butter. Stir and saute until vegetables are tender-crisp.

- In separate saucepan, cook rice according to package directions.

- In sprayed 10 x 15-inch baking dish, spoon rice over bottom of dish and layer beef mixture, salsa and cheese. Cover and bake for 25 minutes.

- Remove from oven and sprinkle tortilla chips over top. Bake for another 10 to 15 minutes or until chips are light brown. Serves 20.

Where is your faith? Luke 8:25

Spicy Beef and Noodles

This is an ideal casserole to make ahead of time for a quick-and-easy supper. The flavors blend to create a delicious dish that people will remember.

2 pounds lean ground beef
1 large onion, chopped
1 green bell pepper, seeded, chopped
1 (16 ounce) package shredded Mexican Velveeta® cheese
1 (10 ounce) can fiesta nacho cheese soup
1 (15 ounce) can Mexican stewed tomatoes
1 (15 ounce) can whole kernel corn, drained
1 teaspoon chili powder
1 (12 ounce) package medium egg noodles
1 (8 ounce) package shredded cheddar cheese

- Preheat oven to 350°.
- In skillet, cook beef, onion and bell pepper until beef is no longer pink and vegetables are tender. Drain. Remove from heat, add Velveeta® cheese and stir until cheese melts.
- In large mixing bowl, combine fiesta nacho cheese, stewed tomatoes, corn, chili powder and a little salt. Add beef mixture and mix well.
- Cook egg noodles according to package directions and drain well. Stir noodles into tomato-beef mixture. Transfer to sprayed 10 x 15-inch baking dish.
- Cover and bake for 50 to 55 minutes.
- Uncover and sprinkle cheddar cheese over casserole and return to oven for 5 minutes. Serves 20.

A happy heart makes the face cheerful. Proverbs 15:13

Beef for 20+

Fruit-Covered Pork Loin

1 (4 - 5 pound) pork loin roast
1 teaspoon dried rosemary
1 teaspoon seasoned pepper
¼ cup (½ stick) butter
1 cup orange juice
2 (11 ounce) cans mandarin oranges, drained
1 (16 ounce) can whole berry cranberry sauce
1 (15 ounce) jar apricot preserves
1 (14 ounce) can chicken broth
2 teaspoons red wine vinegar
2 tablespoons white wine Worcestershire sauce
2 cups cooked white rice

- Preheat oven to 350°.
- Place roast in shallow roasting pan. Sprinkle with rosemary and pepper. Bake uncovered for 1 hour.
- In large saucepan, combine remaining ingredients except rice. Bring ingredients to a boil, reduce heat and simmer for 20 minutes.
- Remove roast from oven and spoon about 1 cup sauce over roast. Return to oven and cook additional 1 hour or until meat thermometer registers 165°. Let roast stand for several minutes before slicing.
- Spoon meat juices from roast into remaining fruit sauce and heat. Place cooked rice on large serving platter and place slices of roast over rice. Pour heated sauce in gravy boat and serve with rice and roast. Serves 20.

Let us draw near to God with a sincere heart in full assurance of faith.
Hebrews 10:22

On-the-Border Pork Casserole

This zesty casserole really gets your attention and it is so easy to prepare.
It's a great change from the usual Mexican dish with ground beef.

2 - 2½ pounds pork tenderloin
1 onion, chopped
2 green bell peppers, seeded, chopped
3 tablespoons oil
2 (15 ounce) cans black beans, rinsed, drained
1 (10 ounce) can fiesta nacho cheese soup
1 (15 ounce) can Mexican stewed tomatoes
2 cups instant brown rice, cooked
1 (16 ounce) jar mild salsa
2 teaspoons ground cumin
½ teaspoon garlic powder
1 (12 ounce) package shredded Mexican 3-cheese blend

- Preheat oven to 350°.
- Cut pork into 1-inch cubes. In very large skillet or roasting pan, brown and cook pork, onion and bell peppers in oil until pork is no longer pink. Drain.
- Add beans, nacho cheese soup, stewed tomatoes, rice, salsa, cumin, garlic powder and a little salt. Cook on low-medium heat and stir occasionally until mixture bubbles.
- Spoon into sprayed 10 x 15-inch baking dish. Cover and bake for 40 to 45 minutes.
- Remove from oven and sprinkle with cheese. Return to oven for 5 minutes. Serves 20.

We have this hope as an anchor for the soul, firm and secure.
Hebrews 6:19

Pork, Peas and Pasta

Pork casseroles are not as plentiful as chicken or beef, but just as good.
This pork casserole is a real 'find'.

2 (1 pound) pork tenderloins
2 tablespoons oil, divided
1½ cups sliced celery
1 large onion, chopped
2 red bell peppers, seeded, chopped
1 (12 ounce) package small egg noodles, cooked, drained
1 (10 ounce) can cream of chicken soup
1 (14 ounce) can chicken broth
1 (8 ounce) carton whipping cream
1 (10 ounce) package frozen green peas, thawed
1½ teaspoons seasoned salt
1½ cups seasoned dry breadcrumbs
¾ cup chopped walnuts

- Preheat oven to 325°.

- Cut pork tenderloin into ½-inch cubes. In large skillet, brown pork in 1 tablespoon oil. Reduce heat and cook for about 25 minutes. Remove pork to separate dish.

- Add remaining oil, saute celery, onion and bell peppers.

- Stir in pork, noodles, soup, broth, whipping cream, peas, seasoned salt and 1 teaspoon pepper; mix well. Spoon into sprayed 10 x 15-inch baking dish. Sprinkle with breadcrumbs and walnuts.

- Bake uncovered for 45 to 50 minutes or until bubbly around edges and breadcrumbs are light brown. Serves 20.

A righteous man is cautious in friendship. Proverbs 12:26

Ham-Linguine Special

2 teaspoons minced garlic
¾ cup coarsely chopped walnuts
2 red bell peppers, julienned
1 green bell pepper, julienned
¼ cup olive oil
1 pound cooked ham, cut in strips
1 (16 ounce) jar creamy alfredo sauce
1 (8 ounce) carton sour cream
1 (5 ounce) package grated Parmesan cheese
1 (12 ounce) package shredded mozzarella cheese
1 (12 ounce) package linguine, cooked
1½ cups seasoned breadcrumbs
¼ cup (½ stick) butter, melted

- Preheat oven to 325°.
- In large skillet, saute garlic, walnuts and bell peppers in oil for 1 to 2 minutes.
- In large bowl, combine garlic-bell pepper mixture, ham, alfredo sauce, sour cream, Parmesan cheese and mozzarella cheese; mix well.
- Gently fold in cooked linguine and spoon into sprayed 10 x 15-inch baking dish. Combine breadcrumbs and melted butter and sprinkle over top of casserole.
- Bake uncovered for 40 to 45 minutes or until breadcrumbs are light brown. Serves 20.

You know that the testing of your faith develops perseverance.
James 1:3

Pork for 20+

Salmon Straight from the Pantry

This is canned salmon all dressed up!

1 (10 ounce) package medium egg noodles
1 (10 ounce) can cream of celery soup
1 (10 ounce) can cream of chicken soup
1 (5 ounce) can evaporated milk
2 tablespoons lemon juice
1 onion, finely chopped
2 (15 ounce) cans salmon, drained
1 (8 ounce) package shredded Monterey Jack cheese
1 (8 ounce) can small green peas, drained
1 teaspoon seasoned salt
1 teaspoon Creole seasoning
2 cups crushed cheese crackers
¼ cup (½ stick) butter, melted

- Preheat oven to 325°.
- Cook noodles according to package directions and drain.
- In large bowl, stir in soups, milk, lemon juice and onion. Remove skin and bones from salmon and add to bowl. Stir in cheese, peas, seasoned salt and Creole seasoning.
- Spoon into sprayed 10 x 15-inch baking dish. Cover and bake for 25 minutes.
- Combine cheese crackers and melted butter and sprinkle over casserole. Return to oven for about 15 minutes or until crumbs are light brown. Serves 20.

Do not neglect your gift. First Timothy 4:14

 # Shoe-String Tuna Bake

1 (12 ounce) package egg noodles
2 (10 ounce) cans cream of chicken soup
1 (10 ounce) can cream of celery soup
1 (8 ounce) carton sour cream
2 teaspoons Creole seasoning
¾ cup milk
2 (12 ounce) cans white meat tuna, drained
1 (8 ounce) package shredded Velveeta® cheese
1 (16 ounce) box frozen green peas, thawed
1 (4 ounce) jar diced pimento
2 (1.5 ounce) cans shoe-string potatoes

- Preheat oven to 325°.
- Cook noodles according to package directions and drain.
- In large bowl, combine soups, sour cream, Creole seasoning and milk; mix well. Stir in noodles, tuna, cheese, peas and pimento.
- Pour into sprayed 10 x 15-inch baking dish. Sprinkle top with shoe-string potatoes.
- Bake uncovered for 40 to 45 minutes or until shoe-string potatoes are light brown. Serves 20.

Glorify the Lord with me; let us exalt his name together. Psalm 34:3

Seafood for 20+

Easy Lemon Pound Cake

1 cup butter, softened
½ cup shortening
2¾ cups sugar
5 large eggs, beaten
1 teaspoon lemon extract
¾ cup lemon-lime soda
3 cups flour
Powdered sugar

- Preheat oven to 325°.

- In mixing bowl, beat butter, shortening and sugar about 4 minutes until light and fluffy. Add eggs, one at a time, and beat well after each addition. Add lemon extract and lemon-lime soda alternately with flour.

- Pour into sprayed, floured bundt pan and bake for 1 hour 15 minutes or until toothpick inserted near center comes out clean. Cool about 10 minutes before removing from pan. When cake is completely cool, dust with powdered sugar. Serves 20.

Let your light shine before men, that they may see your good deeds and praise your Father in heaven. Matthew 5:16

Holiday Red Velvet Cake

1 (18 ounce) package German chocolate cake mix
1 (1 ounce) bottle red food coloring
⅓ cup oil
3 eggs, slightly beaten
1 (16 ounce) can white frosting
Small decorative candies and sprinkles

- Preheat oven to 350°.
- Before you measure water called for in cake mix, place red food coloring in cup, then add enough water to make 1⅓ cups.
- Prepare cake mix according to package directions with water, oil and eggs. Pour into 2 (8 or 9 inch) sprayed, floured cake pans.
- Bake for 25 to 30 minutes. Cake is done when toothpick inserted in center comes out clean.
- Frost each layer with white frosting and decorate top layer with tiny red candies. Serves 20.

TIP: Decorative candies are near the cake mixes.

Then we will no longer be infants, tossed back and forth by the waves.
Ephesians 4:14

White Chocolate-Almond Cake

1 (18 ounce) box white cake mix
4 egg whites
¼ cup oil
1 teaspoon almond extract
1 cup slivered almonds, chopped
6 (1 ounce) squares white chocolate, melted
1 (16 ounce) can caramel icing

- Preheat oven to 350°.
- In mixing bowl, combine cake mix, egg whites, oil, almond extract and 1½ cups water; beat until mixture blends well.
- Stir in almonds and melted white chocolate and pour into 2 (9 inch) sprayed, floured round cake pans.
- Bake for 30 to 35 minutes or until toothpick inserted in center comes out clean.
- Spread each layer with half of caramel icing. Place second layer on top of first layer. Serves 20.

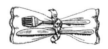

Lead me, O Lord in your righteousness … make straight your way before me.
Psalm 5:8

Special Cherry Dump Cake

1 (20 ounce) can crushed pineapple with juice
1 (20 ounce) can cherry pie filling
1 (18 ounce) box yellow cake mix
¾ cup (1½ sticks) butter, melted
¾ cup flaked coconut
1 cup chopped pecans

- Preheat oven to 350°.
- Spoon pineapple evenly over bottom of unsprayed 9 x 13-inch baking pan; cover evenly with pie filling.
- Sprinkle cake mix evenly over filling and drizzle with melted butter; do not stir. Sprinkle coconut and pecans evenly over cake mix.
- Bake for 55 minutes to 1 hour or until top browns. Serves 20.

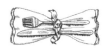

Therefore do not worry about tomorrow, for tomorrow will worry about itself.
Matthew 6:34

Special Topping White Cake

1 (18 ounce) package white cake mix
1 cup graham cracker crumbs
⅓ cup oil
3 eggs
½ cup chopped pecans
1 (16 ounce) jar chocolate ice cream topping, divided
1 (7 ounce) jar marshmallow creme

- Preheat oven to 350°.
- In mixing bowl, beat cake mix, cracker crumbs, 1¼ cups water, oil and eggs with mixer on medium speed for 2 minutes.
- Stir in chopped pecans and pour into sprayed, floured 9 x 13-inch baking pan. Reserve ¼ cup chocolate topping and drop remaining topping by generous tablespoonfuls randomly in 12 to 14 mounds onto batter in pan. Bake for 40 to 45 minutes. Cool 15 minutes.
- Spoon teaspoonfuls of marshmallow creme onto warm cake and carefully spread with knife dipped in hot water. Drop small dollops of reserved chocolate topping randomly over marshmallow creme.
- Swirl topping through marshmallow creme with knife for marbled design. Cool 2 hours before cutting.
- To cut cake easily, use serrated knife and dip in hot water before cutting each piece to keep frosting from sticking. Serves 20.

There is a time to weep and a time to laugh. Ecclesiastes 3:4

Coconut Cupcakes

2 cups flaked coconut
½ cup sweetened condensed milk
1 (18 ounce) package yellow cake mix
⅓ cup oil
3 eggs
1 (16 ounce) can vanilla frosting
1 cup flaked coconut, toasted

- Preheat oven to 375°.

- Place paper baking cups in 24 regular-size muffin cups.
  In medium bowl, combine coconut and sweetened condensed milk and set aside.

- In mixing bowl, beat cake mix, 1¼ cups water, oil and
  eggs with electric mixer on low speed for 30 seconds.
  Beat 2 minutes on medium speed. Divide batter evenly
  among muffin cups and top each cupcake with 1 tablespoon coconut mixture.

- Bake for 18 to 22 minutes or until top springs back when
  lightly touched. Cool completely. Ice each cupcake
  with frosting and dip tops in toasted coconut. Serves
  20 to 24.

*TIP: Toast coconut on baking sheet at 325° for about 5 min-
utes.*

Whoever loves God must also love his brother. First John 4:21

 Blueberry Bounce

1½ cups quick-cooking oats
2 cups packed brown sugar
1 (20 ounce) can blueberry pie filling
1 (18 ounce) box yellow cake mix
¾ cup chopped pecans
½ cup (1 stick) butter, melted

- Preheat oven to 350°.
- Spray 9 x 13-inch glass baking dish. In medium bowl, combine oats and brown sugar and sprinkle half in bottom of baking dish.
- Spoon blueberry pie filling over oat-sugar mixture and spread evenly. Crumble cake mix over filling and spread evenly.
- Combine pecans with remaining oat mixture and sprinkle over cake mix. Drizzle butter evenly across oat-sugar mixture and bake for 35 to 40 minutes or until brown sugar looks like caramel. Serves 20.

Let us draw near to God with a sincere heart in full assurance of faith.
Hebrews 10:22

Index

A

A Deal of a Chicken Bake 222
A Different Macaroni 154
A Touch of Mexico 228
Alfredo Salmon and Noodles 189
Alfredo-Chicken Spaghetti 67
Almond-Crusted Chicken 63

Appetizers

Cheesy Vegetable Squares 11
Chili-Honey Wings 12
Orange-Glazed Chicken Wings 12
Apple Crescents 38
Apple Crumble 170
Artichoke Fettuccine 158
Asparagus Casserole 125
Awesome Sweet Potatoes 219

B

Baked Cauliflower 130
Baked Chicken and Mushrooms 78
Baked Potato Supper 152
Baked Turkey and Dressing 83
Barbecue Chicken Salad 72
Barbecue Pizza 181

Beef

Barbecue Pizza 181
Beef Patties in Onion Sauce 84
Beef-Onion Casserole 180
Beef-Potato Casserole 85
Beefy-Rice Casserole 84
Black Bean Chili Casserole 86
Cheesy Meatball Pie 92
Classy Beef and Noodles 96
Creamy Beef Casserole 87
Creamy Onion-Beef Patties 181
Dinner with the Italian Touch 227
Dutch-Oven Roast 96
Good Night Casserole Supper 88
Meatloaf Tonight 85
Quick Skillet Supper 182
Rueben Casserole Supper 97
Savory Beef Patties 88
Shepherd's Pie 95
Sirloin in Rich Mushroom Sauce 182
Smothered Steak 180
Smothered Steak and Potatoes 94

Southern Taco Pie 89
Speedy Steak Strombolis 183
Spicy Beef and Noodles 229
Spicy Onion-Mushroom Steak 94
Taco Pie 91
Tasty Taco Casserole 93
Tex-Mex Supper 90
Thai Beef, Noodle and Veggies 183
Beef Patties in Onion Sauce 84
Beef-Onion Casserole 180
Beef-Potato Casserole 85
Beefy-Rice Casserole 84

Beverages

Green Party Punch 8
Holiday Party Punch 9
Reception Punch 9
Ruby Holiday Punch 10
Sparkling Cranberry Punch 10
Very Special Coffee Punch 8
Black Bean & Mandarin Salad 16
Black Bean Chili Casserole 86
Black-Eyed Peas and Ham 148
Blueberry Bounce 242
Blueberry Cobbler 169

Breads

Buttered Ranch Style Bread 120
Cheddar-Tomato Bread 199
Cheese Bread 201
Cheese-Toasted French Bread 119
Cheesy Breadsticks 119
Corny Sausage Squares 118
Creamy Rich Biscuits 124
Crunch Corn Sticks 118
Deluxe Parmesan Bread 115
French Cheese Loaf 200
Garlic Rounds 200
Green Chile-Cheese Bread 117
Herb Pull-Apart Bread 121
Holiday Bread 122
Jack's Breadsticks 201
Lariat Bread Knots 199
Monterey Breadsticks 115
Quick Onion Biscuits 124
Seasoned Breadsticks 114
Sour Cream Biscuits 123

Sticky Sweet Rolls 116
Supper Biscuits 123
Swiss Bread Slices 120
Texas Cornbread 117
Broccoli Frittata 127
Broccoli -Rice and Ham Supper 97
Broccoli Slaw 35
Broccoli-Cauliflower Casserole 129
Brown Rice Chicken Salad 30
Brown Sugar Carrots 191
Buttered Ranch-Style Bread 120

C
Cabbage-Carrot Slaw 35

Cakes
Caramel-Coconut Cake 162
Coconut Cupcakes 241
Easy Lemon Pound Cake 236
Extreme Pound Cake 210
Holiday Red Velvet Cake 237
Lemon Poppy Seed Cake 164
Nutmeg Cake 163
Quick Summer Cake 210
Special Cherry Dump Cake 239
Special Topping White Cake 240
White Chocolate-Almond Cake 238

Caramel-Coconut Cake 162
Carnival Couscous 198
Carrot Apple Salad 202
Carrots Bring Sunshine 214
Cashew Chicken and Veggies 62
Cauliflower-Bacon Salad 17
Cheddar-Broccoli Bake 126
Cheddar-Tomato Bread 199
Cheese Bread 201
Cheesecake Squares 38
Cheese-Toasted French Bread 119
Cheesy Baked Onions 194
Cheesy Black Olive Sandwiches 13
Cheesy Breadsticks 119
Cheesy Broccoli-Rice Bake 217
Cheesy Chicken Noodles 223
Cheesy Chicken Pie 61
Cheesy Crusted Chicken 172
Cheesy Grits Bake 161
Cheesy Meatball Pie 92

Cheesy New Potatoes 197
Cheesy Noodle Casserole 157
Cheesy Summer Squash 191
Cheesy Vegetable Salad 207
Cheesy Vegetable Squares 11
Cherry Crush 204
Cherry-Cranberry Salad 206

Chicken
A Deal of a Chicken Bake 222
Alfredo-Chicken Spaghetti 67
Almond-Crusted Chicken 63
Baked Chicken and Mushrooms 78
Baked Turkey and Dressing 83
Barbecue Chicken Salad 72
Brown Rice Chicken Salad 30
Cashew Chicken and Veggies 62
Cheesy Chicken Noodles 223
Cheesy Chicken Pie 61
Cheesy Crusted Chicken 172
Chicken a la Orange 60
Chicken and Potatoes 56
Chicken and Stuffing Bake 78
Chicken Couscous 75
Chicken Lasagna 76
Chicken Linguine 65
Chicken on the Ranch 80
Chicken Squares 73
Chicken-Bacon Sandwiches 14
Chicken-Broccoli Bake 79
Chicken-Green Bean Bake 72
Chicken-Sausage Casserole 77
Chicken-Spaghetti Bake 74
Chicken-Taco Pie 64
Chicken-Waldorf Salad 31
Chili-Honey Wings 12
Chop Suey Veggies and Chicken 71
Confetti Squash and Chicken 70
Cranberry Chicken 172
Cranberry-Turkey and Stuffing 82
Creamy Chicken and Broccoli 173
Creamy Tarragon Chicken 58
Crispy Nutty Chicken Breasts 173
Crunchy Baked Chicken 53
Crunchy Chicken Breasts 174
Encore Chicken 56

Index

Fiesta Time for Chicken 224
Glazed Chicken Over Rice 53
Great Chicken 'N Greens Salad 22
Green Chile-Chicken Casserole 59
Honey-Glazed Chicken 55
Imperial Chicken Casserole 52
Marinated Salsa Chicken 54
Mozzarella Chicken Breasts 175
Mushroom-Onion Chicken 175
Mushrooms, Noodles and Chicken 57
Noodle-Turkey Salad 205
Orange Chicken Over Rice 52
Orange-Glazed Chicken Wings 12
Parmesan Chicken 176
Party Chicken 66
Pimento Cheese-Stuffed Fried Chicken 51
Quick Chicken Supper 69
Ranch Chicken To Go 69
Requested Favorite Chicken 176
Roasted Chicken 179
Rolled Chicken Florentine 50
Sassy Chicken Over Tex-Mex Corn 46
Saucy Chicken 174
Spaghetti Toss 66
Spicy Orange Chicken Over Noodles 49
Supper-Ready Chicken 47
Supper-Ready Limeade Chicken 177
Supreme Chicken and Green Beans 68
Sweet'n Spicy Chicken 47
Sweet-Spicy Chicken Thighs 177
Taco Chicken Over Spanish Rice 48
Tempting Chicken 179
Turkey and Noodles Plus 82
Turkey and Rice Supper 81
Turkey and the Works 178
Turkey on a Muffin 15
Turkey-Apple Salad 32
Turkey-Black Bean Salad 33
Turkey-Cranberry Croissants 15
Turkey-Stuffing Casserole 81
Veggie Cheesy Chicken 225
Walnuts Make the Chicken 226
Chicken a la Orange 60
Chicken and Potatoes 56
Chicken and Stuffing Bake 78

Chicken Couscous 75
Chicken Lasagna 76
Chicken Linguine 65
Chicken on the Ranch 80
Chicken Squares 73
Chicken-Bacon Sandwiches 14
Chicken-Broccoli Bake 79
Chicken-Green Bean Bake 72
Chicken-Sausage Casserole 77
Chicken-Spaghetti Bake 74
Chicken-Taco Pie 64
Chicken-Waldorf Salad 31
Chili-Baked Beans 190
Chili-Honey Wings 12
Chilled Cinnamon Salad 32
Chocolate Bread Pudding 44
Chocolate-Caramel Pie 167
Chocolate-Fudge Brownies 37
Chocolate-Pecan Chess Pie 165
Choice Broccoli-Swiss Salad 17
Choice Tenderloin Slices 105
Chop Suey Veggies and Chicken 71
Cinnamon Baked Apples 198
Citrus-Broccoli Slaw 36
Classic Apple-Cranberry Salad 19
Classy Beef and Noodles 96
Coconut Cupcakes 241
Colorful English Pea Salad 16
Colorful Sausage Supper 111
Confetti Squash and Chicken 70
Corn Success 211
Corn That Pleases 213
Corny Sausage Squares 118
Couscous and Veggies 157
Couscous Salad 20
Cranberries Supreme 220
Cranberry Chicken 172
Cranberry-Cherry Salad 34
Cranberry-Turkey and Stuffing 82
Creamed Asparagus 192
Creamed Onions and Peas 133
Creamed Vegetable Bake 134
Creamy Beef Casserole 87
Creamy Cauliflower 193

Index

Creamy Chicken and Broccoli 173
Creamy Onion-Beef Patties 181
Creamy Pumpkin Pie 166
Creamy Ranch Potatoes 151
Creamy Rich Biscuits 124
Creamy Spinach To Love 215
Creamy Tarragon Chicken 58
Creamy, Cheesy Spaghetti Chicken 221
Creamy-Cheesy Zucchini 135
Crispy Nutty Chicken Breasts 173
Crunch Corn Sticks 118
Crunchy Baked Chicken 53
Crunchy Chicken Breasts 174
Crunchy Pork Chops 105
Cucumber-Onion Salad 207

D

Decadent Oatmeal Cookies 42
Deluxe Parmesan Bread 115

Desserts

Apple Crescents 38
Apple Crumble 170
Blueberry Bounce 242
Blueberry Cobbler 169
Caramel Coconut Cake 162
Cheesecake Squares 38
Chocolate Bread Pudding 44
Chocolate-Caramel Pie 167
Chocolate-Fudge Brownies 37
Chocolate-Pecan Chess Pie 165
Coconut Cupcakes 241
Creamy Pumpkin Pie 166
Decadent Oatmeal Cookies 42
Dreamy-Creamy Dessert 208
Easy Lemon Pound Cake 236
Extreme Pound Cake 210
Fruit Crispy 44
Fruit Medley 209
Holiday Red Velvet Cake 237
Lemon Poppy Seed Cake 164
Luscious Strawberry Pie 167
Nutmeg Cake 163
Peanut Brittle Bars 40
Peanut Butter Drops 208
Peanut Butter-Toffee Bars 39
Pecan Squares 41

Pecan Tassies 43
Quick Summer Cake 210
Special Cherry Dump Cake 239
Special Topping White Cake 240
Thanksgiving Pie 168
Walnut Squares 209
White Chocolate-Almond Cake 238

Deviled Eggs 25
Dinner with the Italian Touch 227
Dreamy-Creamy Dessert 208
Dutch-Oven Roast 96

E

Easy Lemon Pound Cake 236
Encore Chicken 56
Everybody's Favorite Corn 133
Extreme Pound Cake 210

F

Fancy Green Beans 137
Favorite Fettuccine 195
Festive Cranberry Salad 202
Festive Green and Yellow Veggie Salad 203
Fiesta Corn 132
Fiesta Time for Chicken 224
Filled Summer Squash 138
French Cheese Loaf 200
Fruit Covered Pork Loin 230
Fruit Crispy 44
Fruit Medley 209

G

Garden Casserole 139
Garlic Rounds 200
Garlic-Roasted Pork Tenderloin 107
Glazed Chicken Over Rice 53
Good Night Casserole Supper 88
Great Carrot Salad 18
Great Chicken 'N Greens Salad 22
Green Caesar Bake 136
Green Chile-Cheese Bread 117
Green Chile-Chicken Casserole 59
Green Party Punch 8
Green Salad with Candied Pecans 21
Guacamole-Ham Wrap 13

H

Ham and Corn Casserole 101
Ham and Pasta Bake 102

Index

Ham and Veggies 188
Ham for a Bunch 99
Ham Supper Quick 98
Ham-Linguine Special 233
Ham-Vegetable Supper 100
Hearty Maple Beans 147
Herb Pull-Apart Bread 121
Holiday Bread 122
Holiday Party Punch 9
Holiday Red Velvet Cake 237
Honey-Glazed Chicken 55

I
Imperial Chicken Casserole 52
Impossible Broccoli Pie 128
Instant Beans and Rice 197
Italian White Beans 138
Italian-Style Rice and Beans 158

J
Jack's Breadsticks 201
Jazzy Cheesy Broccoli 126

L
Lariat Bread Knots 199
Lemon Poppy Seed Cake 164
Lucky Black-Eyed Peas 148
Luscious Strawberry Pie 167

M
Mac 'n Cheese Casserole 98
Macaroni and Cheese Deluxe 155
Macaroni-Vegetable Salad 18

Main Dishes
A Deal of a Chicken Bake 222
A Touch of Mexico 228
Alfredo Salmon and Noodles 189
Alfredo-Chicken Spaghetti 67
Almond-Crusted Chicken 63
Baked Chicken and Mushrooms 78
Baked Turkey and Dressing 83
Barbecue Chicken Salad 72
Barbecue Pizza 181
Beef Patties in Onion Sauce 84
Beef-Onion Casserole 180
Beef-Potato Casserole 85
Beefy-Rice Casserole 84
Black Bean Chili Casserole 86
Broccoli -Rice and Ham Supper 97

Cashew Chicken and Veggies 62
Cheesy Chicken Noodles 223
Cheesy Chicken Pie 61
Cheesy Crusted Chicken 172
Cheesy Meatball Pie 92
Chicken a la Orange 60
Chicken and Potatoes 56
Chicken and Stuffing Bake 78
Chicken Couscous 75
Chicken Lasagna 76
Chicken Linguine 65
Chicken on the Ranch 80
Chicken Squares 73
Chicken-Broccoli Bake 79
Chicken-Green Bean Bake 72
Chicken-Sausage Casserole 77
Chicken-Spaghetti Bake 74
Chicken-Taco Pie 64
Choice Tenderloin Slices 105
Chop Suey Veggies and Chicken 71
Classy Beef and Noodles 96
Colorful Sausage Supper 111
Confetti Squash and Chicken 70
Cranberry Chicken 172
Cranberry-Turkey and Stuffing 82
Creamy Beef Casserole 87
Creamy Chicken and Broccoli 173
Creamy Onion-Beef Patties 181
Creamy Tarragon Chicken 58
Crispy Nutty Chicken Breasts 173
Crunchy Baked Chicken 53
Crunchy Chicken Breasts 174
Crunchy Pork Chops 105
Dinner with the Italian Touch 227
Dutch-Oven Roast 96
Encore Chicken 56
Fiesta Time for Chicken 224
Fruit Covered Pork Loin 230
Garlic-Roasted Pork Tenderloin 107
Glazed Chicken Over Rice 53
Good Night Casserole Supper 88
Green Chile-Chicken Casserole 59
Ham and Corn Casserole 101
Ham and Pasta Bake 102
Ham and Veggies 188

Index

Ham for a Bunch 99
Ham Supper Quick 98
Ham-Linguine Special 233
Ham-Vegetable Supper 100
Honey-Glazed Chicken 55
Imperial Chicken Casserole 52
Mac 'n Cheese Casserole 98
Marinated Salsa Chicken 54
Meatloaf Tonight 85
Mozzarella Chicken Breasts 175
Mushroom-Onion Chicken 175
Mushrooms, Noodles and Chicken 57
Nutty Pork Loin 108
On the Border Pork Casserole 231
Orange Chicken Over Rice 52
Orange Pork Chops 188
Parmesan Chicken 176
Party Chicken 66
Pimento Cheese-Stuffed Fried Chicken 51
Pork Chop Supper 187
Pork Chops and Potatoes 103
Pork Chops Deluxe 109
Pork, Peas and Pasta 232
Quick Chicken Supper 69
Quick Skillet Supper 182
Ranch Chicken To Go 69
Ravioli and Tomatoes 187
Requested Favorite Chicken 176
Roasted Chicken 179
Rolled Chicken Florentine 50
Rueben Casserole Supper 97
Salmon Straight from the Pantry 234
Sassy Chicken Over Tex-Mex Corn 46
Saucy Chicken 174
Sausage-Bean Casserole 110
Sausage-Potato Bake 110
Savory Beef Patties 88
Savory Pork Chops 184
Savory Sauce Over Pork Tenderloin 185
Shepherd's Pie 95
Shoe-String Tuna Bake 235
Shrimp and Chicken Curry 113
Shrimp and Crab Casserole 189
Sirloin in Rich Mushroom Sauce 182
Smothered Steak 180

Smothered Steak and Potatoes 94
Southern Taco Pie 89
Spaghetti Toss 66
Speedy Steak Strombolis 183
Spicy Beef and Noodles 229
Spicy Glazed Pork Tenderloin 106
Spicy Onion-Mushroom Steak 94
Spicy Orange Chicken Over Noodles 49
Stuffed Pork Chops 104
Stuffing Over Pork Chops 185
Supper-Ready Chicken 47
Supper-Ready Limeade Chicken 177
Supreme Chicken and Green Beans 68
Sweet and Sour Pork Chops 103
Sweet and Sour Pork Loin Roast 112
Sweet Peach Pork Tenderloin 184
Sweet Potato Ham 186
Sweet'n Spicy Chicken 47
Sweet-Spicy Chicken Thighs 177
Taco Chicken Over Spanish Rice 48
Taco Pie 91
Tasty Taco Casserole 93
Tempting Chicken 179
Tex-Mex Supper 90
Thai Beef, Noodle and Veggies 183
Tortellini-Ham Supper 186
Tuna-Pasta Casserole 114
Tuna-Stuffed Tomatoes 113
Turkey and Noodles Plus 82
Turkey and Rice Supper 81
Turkey and the Works 178
Turkey-Stuffing Casserole 81
Veggie Cheesy Chicken 225
Walnuts Make the Chicken 226
Mandarin Fluff 206
Mango Salad Supreme 34
Maple-Pecan Sweet Potatoes 195
Maple-Raisin Carrots 131
Marinated Salsa Chicken 54
Meatloaf Tonight 85
Monterey Breadsticks 115
Mozzarella Chicken Breasts 175
Mushroom-Onion Chicken 175
Mushrooms, Noodles and Chicken 57

Index

N

Noodle-Turkey Salad 205
No-Trouble Fruit Salad 33
Nutmeg Cake 163
Nutty Pork Loin 108
Nutty Rice Salad 23

O

On the Border Pork Casserole 231
Orange Chicken Over Rice 52
Orange Glow 205
Orange Pork Chops 188
Orange-Cranberry Salad 20
Orange-Glazed Chicken Wings 12
Oriental Spinach Salad 27
Oven-Baked Asparagus 192

P

Parmesan Chicken 176
Parmesan-Garlic Orzo 160
Party Chicken 66
Party Sandwich Strips 14
Pasta Plus Salad 24
Pasta -Veggie Salad 24
Peanut Brittle Bars 40
Peanut Butter Drops 208
Peanut Butter-Toffee Bars 39
Pecan Squares 41
Pecan Tassies 43
Pecan-Mushroom Rice 161

Pies

Apple Crumble 170
Blueberry Bounce 242
Blueberry Cobbler 169
Chocolate-Caramel Pie 167
Chocolate-Pecan Chess Pie 165
Creamy Pumpkin Pie 166
Luscious Strawberry Pie 167
Thanksgiving Pie 168
Pimento Cheese-Stuffed Fried Chicken 51

Pork

Broccoli -Rice and Ham Supper 97
Cauliflower-Bacon Salad 17
Chicken-Bacon Sandwiches 14
Choice Tenderloin Slices 105
Colorful Sausage Supper 111
Crunchy Pork Chops 105
Fruit Covered Pork Loin 230
Garlic-Roasted Pork Tenderloin 107
Ham and Corn Casserole 101
Ham and Pasta Bake 102
Ham and Veggies 188
Ham for a Bunch 99
Ham Supper Quick 98
Ham-Linguine Special 233
Ham-Vegetable Supper 100
Mac 'n Cheese Casserole 98
Nutty Pork Loin 108
On the Border Pork Casserole 231
Orange Pork Chops 188
Party Sandwich Strips 14
Pork Chop Supper 187
Pork Chops and Potatoes 103
Pork Chops Deluxe 109
Pork, Peas and Pasta 232
Ravioli and Tomatoes 187
Sausage-Bean Casserole 110
Sausage-Potato Bake 110
Savory Pork Chops 184
Savory Sauce Over Pork Tenderloin 185
Spicy Glazed Pork Tenderloin 106
Spinach Salad w/ Warm Bacon Dressing 28
Stuffed Pork Chops 104
Stuffing Over Pork Chops 185
Sweet and Sour Pork Chops 103
Sweet and Sour Pork Loin Roast 112
Sweet Peach Pork Tenderloin 184
Sweet Potato Ham 186
Tortellini-Ham Supper 186
Pork Chop Supper 187
Pork Chops and Potatoes 103
Pork Chops Deluxe 109
Pork, Peas and Pasta 232
Potato Supreme 218
Potato-Stuffed Bell Peppers 145

Q

Quick Chicken Supper 69
Quick Onion Biscuits 124
Quick Potato Salad 204
Quick Skillet Supper 182
Quick Summer Cake 210

R

Ranch Chicken To Go 69
Ranch Potato Salad 30
Ranch Spaghetti 160
Ravioli and Tomatoes 187
Reception Punch 9
Requested Favorite Chicken 176
Roasted Chicken 179
Rolled Chicken Florentine 50
Ruby Holiday Punch 10
Rueben Casserole Supper 97

S

Salads

Black Bean & Mandarin Salad 16
Broccoli Slaw 35
Brown Rice Chicken Salad 30
Cabbage-Carrot Slaw 35
Carrot Apple Salad 202
Cauliflower-Bacon Salad 17
Cheesy Vegetable Salad 207
Cherry Crush 204
Cherry-Cranberry Salad 206
Chicken-Waldorf Salad 31
Chilled Cinnamon Salad 32
Choice Broccoli-Swiss Salad 17
Citrus-Broccoli Slaw 36
Classic Apple-Cranberry Salad 19
Colorful English Pea Salad 16
Couscous Salad 20
Cranberry-Cherry Salad 34
Cucumber-Onion Salad 207
Deviled Eggs 25
Festive Cranberry Salad 202
Festive Green and Yellow Veggie Salad 203
Great Carrot Salad 18
Great Chicken 'N Greens Salad 22
Green Salad with Candied Pecans 21
Macaroni-Vegetable Salad 18
Mandarin Fluff 206
Mango Salad Supreme 34
Noodle-Turkey Salad 205
No-Trouble Fruit Salad 33
Nutty Rice Salad 23
Orange Glow 205
Orange-Cranberry Salad 20

Oriental Spinach Salad 27
Pasta Plus Salad 24
Pasta -Veggie Salad 24
Quick Potato Salad 204
Ranch Potato Salad 30
Special Cauliflower Salad 29
Special Macaroni Salad 203
Special Romaine Salad 31
Spinach Salad with Warm Bacon Dressing
Spinach-Strawberry Salad 22
Swiss Romaine 29
Tri-Colored Pasta Salad 25
Turkey-Apple Salad 32
Turkey-Black Bean Salad 33
Zesty Bean Salad 26

Salmon Straight from the Pantry 234

Sandwiches

Cheesy Black Olive Sandwiches 13
Guacamole-Ham Wrap 13
Chicken-Bacon Sandwiches 14
Party Sandwich Strips 14
Turkey on a Muffin 15
Turkey-Cranberry Croissants 15

Saucy Chicken 174
Sausage-Bean Casserole 110
Sausage-Potato Bake 110
Savory Beef Patties 88
Savory Pork Chops 184
Savory Sauce Over Pork Tenderloin 185
Scalloped Cabbage 190

Seafood

Alfredo Salmon and Noodles 189
Salmon Straight from the Pantry 234
Shoe-String Tuna Bake 235
Shrimp and Chicken Curry 113
Shrimp and Crab Casserole 189
Tuna-Pasta Casserole 114
Tuna-Stuffed Tomatoes 113

Seasoned Breadsticks 114
Shepherd's Pie 95
Shoe-String Tuna Bake 235
Shrimp and Chicken Curry 113
Shrimp and Crab Casserole 189

Side Dishes

A Different Macaroni 154

Index

Artichoke Fettuccine 158
Awesome Sweet Potatoes 219
Baked Potato Supper 152
Black-Eyed Peas and Ham 148
Carnival Couscous 198
Cheesy Grits Bake 161
Cheesy New Potatoes 197
Cheesy Noodle Casserole 157
Cinnamon Baked Apples 198
Couscous and Veggies 157
Cranberries Supreme 220
Creamy Ranch Potatoes 151
Creamy, Cheesy Spaghetti Chicken 221
Favorite Fettuccine 195
Hearty Maple Beans 147
Instant Beans and Rice 197
Italian-Style Rice and Beans 158
Lucky Black-Eyed Peas 148
Macaroni and Cheese Deluxe 155
Maple-Pecan Sweet Potatoes 195
Parmesan-Garlic Orzo 160
Pecan-Mushroom Rice 161
Potato Supreme 218
Ranch Spaghetti 160
Southern Hoppin' John 149
Spice Up The Macaroni 156
Supper Frittata 159
Supreme Mashed Potatoes 149
Sweet Potato Bake 152
Sweet Potato Casserole 154
Sweet Potato-Pineapple Bake 153
Tasty Rice Bake 196
The Perfect Potato 151
Whipped Potato Bake 150
Wonderful Alfredo Fettuccine 196
Worth It Macaroni 155
Simply Sweet Carrots 193
Sirloin in Rich Mushroom Sauce 182
Smothered Steak 180
Smothered Steak and Potatoes 94
Sour Cream Biscuits 123
Southern Hoppin' John 149
Southern Taco Pie 89
Spaghetti Toss 66
Sparkling Cranberry Punch 10

Special Cauliflower Salad 29
Special Cherry Dump Cake 239
Special Macaroni Salad 203
Special Romaine Salad 31
Special Topping White Cake 240
Speedy Steak Strombolis 183
Speedy Zucchini and Fettuccine 140
Spice Up The Macaroni 156
Spicy Beef and Noodles 229
Spicy Glazed Pork Tenderloin 106
Spicy Onion-Mushroom Steak 94
Spicy Orange Chicken Over Noodles 49
Spinach Artichoke Bake 143
Spinach Enchiladas 144
Spinach Salad with Warm Bacon Dressing 28
Spinach-Artichoke Special 141
Spinach-Strawberry Salad 22
Sticky Sweet Rolls 116
Stuffed Pork Chops 104
Stuffing Over Pork Chops 185
Sunday Green Beans 136
Sunny Day Carrots 131
Super Spinach Bake 142
Supper Biscuits 123
Supper Frittata 159
Supper-Ready Chicken 47
Supper-Ready Limeade Chicken 177
Supreme Chicken and Green Beans 68
Supreme Mashed Potatoes 149
Swect and Sour Pork Chops 103
Sweet and Sour Pork Loin Roast 112
Sweet Peach Pork Tenderloin 184
Sweet Potato Bake 152
Sweet Potato Casserole 154
Sweet Potato Ham 186
Sweet Potato-Pineapple Bake 153
Sweet'n Spicy Chicken 47
Sweet-Spicy Chicken Thighs 177
Swiss Bread Slices 120
Swiss Romaine 29

T

Taco Chicken Over Spanish Rice 48
Taco Pie 91
Tasty Rice Bake 196
Tasty Taco Casserole 93

Index

Tempting Chicken 179
Texas Cornbread 117
Tex-Mex Supper 90
Thai Beef, Noodle and Veggies 183
Thanksgiving Pie 168
The Perfect Potato 151
Tortellini-Ham Supper 186
Tri-Colored Pasta Salad 25
Tuna-Pasta Casserole 114
Tuna-Stuffed Tomatoes 113
Turkey and Noodles Plus 82
Turkey and Rice Supper 81
Turkey and the Works 178
Turkey on a Muffin 15
Turkey-Apple Salad 32
Turkey-Black Bean Salad 33
Turkey-Cranberry Croissants 15
Turkey-Stuffing Casserole 81

V

Vegetables

Asparagus Casserole 125
Baked Cauliflower 130
Broccoli Frittata 127
Broccoli-Cauliflower Casserole 129
Brown Sugar Carrots 191
Carrots Bring Sunshine 214
Cheddar-Broccoli Bake 126
Cheesy Baked Onions 194
Cheesy Broccoli-Rice Bake 217
Cheesy Summer Squash 191
Chili-Baked Beans 190
Corn Success 211
Corn That Pleases 213
Creamed Asparagus 192
Creamed Onions and Peas 133
Creamed Vegetable Bake 134
Creamy Cauliflower 193
Creamy Spinach To Love 215
Creamy-Cheesy Zucchini 135
Everybody's Favorite Corn 133
Fancy Green Beans 137
Fiesta Corn 132
Filled Summer Squash 138
Garden Casserole 139
Green Caesar Bake 136

Impossible Broccoli Pie 128
Italian White Beans 138
Jazzy Cheesy Broccoli 126
Maple-Raisin Carrots 131
Oven-Baked Asparagus 192
Potato-Stuffed Bell Peppers 145
Scalloped Cabbage 190
Simply Sweet Carrots 193
Speedy Zucchini and Fettuccine 140
Spinach Artichoke Bake 143
Spinach Enchiladas 144
Spinach-Artichoke Special 141
Sunday Green Beans 136
Sunny Day Carrots 131
Super Spinach Bake 142
Vegetables You'll Remember 146
Yellow Squash Deluxe 216
Zucchini and Creamy Penne 194

Vegetables You'll Remember 146
Veggie Cheesy Chicken 225
Very Special Coffee Punch 8

W

Walnut Squares 209
Walnuts Make the Chicken 226
Whipped Potato Bake 150
White Chocolate-Almond Cake 238
Wonderful Alfredo Fettuccine 196
Worth It Macaroni 155

Y

Yellow Squash Deluxe 216

Z

Zesty Bean Salad 26
Zucchini and Creamy Penne 194

Cookbook Resources, LLC
Bringing Families and Friends To The Table

The Best of Cooking with
3 Ingredients

The Ultimate Cooking with
4 Ingredients

Easy Cooking with 5 Ingredients

Diabetic Cooking with
4 Ingredients

Healthy Cooking with 4 Ingredients

Gourmet Cooking with
5 Ingredients

4-Ingredient Recipes for
30-Minute Meals

Essential 3-4-5 Ingredient Recipes

The Best 1001 Short, Easy Recipes

The Best 1001 Fast Easy Recipes

Easy Slow Cooker Cookbook

Easy One-Dish Meals

Easy Potluck Recipes

Easy Casseroles

Easy Desserts

Sunday Night Suppers

365 Easy Meals

365 Easy Chicken Recipes

365 Easy Soups and Stews

Quick Fixes with Cake Mixes

Kitchen Keepsakes/
More Kitchen Keepsakes

Gifts for the Cookie Jar

All New Gifts for the Cookie Jar

The Ultimate Gifts for the Cookie Jar

Muffins In A Jar

Brownies In A Jar

Gifts in a Pickle Jar

The Big Bake Sale Cookbook

Classic Tex-Mex and
Texas Cooking

Classic Southwest Cooking

Southern Family Favorites

Miss Sadie's Southern Cooking

The Great Canadian Cookbook

Texas Longhorn Cookbook

Cookbook 25 Years

The Best of Lone Star Legacy
Cookbook

A Little Taste of Texas

A Little Taste of Texas II

Trophy Hunters'
Wild Game Cookbook

Italian Family Cookbook

Old-Fashioned Cookies

Grandmother's Cookies

Quilters' Cooking Companion

Mother's Recipes

Recipe Keeper

Cookie Dough Secrets

Casseroles to the Rescue

Holiday Recipes

Mealtimes and Memories

Southwest Sizzler

Southwest Olé

Class Treats

Leaving Home

cookbook
resources LLC
www.cookbookresources.com
Your Ultimate Source For Easy Cookbooks

To Order: *Easy Church Suppers*

Please send_____ paperback copies @ $16.95 (U.S.) each $ _____
           Texas residents add sales tax @ $1.40 each $ _____
           Plus postage/handling @ $6.00 (1st copy) $ _____
           $1.00 (each additional copy) $ _____

Check or Credit Card (Canada: Credit card only)**Total** $ _____

Charge to:
_____ MasterCard _____Visa
Account # _____
Expiration Date _____
Signature_____

| **Mail or Call:** |
| Cookbook Resources |
| 541 Doubletree Drive |
| Highland Village, TX 75077 |
| Toll Free (866) 229-2665 |
| Fax   (972) 317-6404 |

Name _____
Address_____
City_____State_____Zip_____
Telephone (Day)_____(Evening)_____

To Order: *Easy Church Suppers*

Please send_____ paperback copies @ $16.95 (U.S.) each $ _____
           Texas residents add sales tax @ $1.40 each $ _____
           Plus postage/handling @ $6.00 (1st copy) $ _____
           $1.00 (each additional copy) $ _____

Check or Credit Card (Canada: Credit card only) **Total** $ _____

Charge to:
_____ MasterCard _____Visa
Account # _____
Expiration Date _____
Signature_____

| **Mail or Call:** |
| Cookbook Resources |
| 541 Doubletree Drive |
| Highland Village, TX 75077 |
| Toll Free (866) 229-2665 |
| Fax   (972) 317-6404 |

Name _____
Address_____
City_____State_____Zip_____
Telephone (Day)_____(Evening)_____

Order online at www.cookbookresources.com